MW00398715

The Nude Beach Notebook

Also by Barbara J. Scot

The Violet Shyness of Their Eyes: Notes from Nepal

Prairie Reunion

The Stations of Still Creek

Child of Steens Mountain with Eileen McVicker

The Nude Beach Notebook

Barbara J. Scot

Barbara Scot (signature)

Oregon State University Press
Corvallis

The paper in this book meets the guidelines for permanence and durability of the Committee on Production Guidelines for Book Longevity of the Council on Library Resources and the minimum requirements of the American National Standard for Permanence of Paper for Printed Library Materials Z39.48-1984.

Library of Congress Cataloging-in-Publication Data
Scot, Barbara J.
  The nude beach notebook / Barbara J. Scot
     pages cm
  ISBN 978-0-87071-740-6 (alk. paper) — ISBN 978-0-87071-741-3 (e-book)
1. Scot, Barbara J.—Travel—Oregon—Sauvie Island. 2. Sauvie Island (Or.)—Description and travel. 3. Walking—Oregon—Sauvie Island. 4. Sauvie Island (Or.)—History. 5. Natural history—Oregon—Sauvie Island. 6. Nude Beaches—Oregon—Sauvie Island. 7. Sauvie Island (Or.)—Social life and customs. 8. Scot, Barbara J., 1942—Family. 9. Brothers and sisters. I. Title.
  F882.S3S36 2014
  979.5'49—dc23
                              2013046083

© 2014 Barbara J. Scot
All rights reserved.
First published in 2014 by Oregon State University Press
Printed in the United States of America

Oregon State University Press
121 The Valley Library
Corvallis OR 97331-4501
541-737-3166 • fax 541-737-3170
www.osupress.oregonstate.edu

This book is dedicated to Charles K. Cannon, professor emeritus, Coe College, Cedar Rapids, Iowa. Dr. Cannon believed in my writing and encouraged me for over fifty years.

Estrangement and reconciliation thread their way through almost every episode in this narrative, as I strive to understand what constitutes and defines family and how to reconcile childhood religious training with adult skepticism. Symbolism presented early in life made a deep imprint on my mind. Sauvie Island and especially the Nude Beach constitute for me a sort of lost Eden with overlays of culture and history, and the Columbia River is the Jordan across which we stare into the blue-gray mists, searching for shades on the other shore. The Odd Ones of the beach are representative of the general mix of humanity: the good, the bad, and the misunderstood. Memory is an unreliable and self-serving medium, certainly by the time one approaches the Biblical allotment of threescore years and ten. Real life is not fiction, but nonfiction, replete with mysteries that can never be fully resolved, but when we follow the thread back to the start of the tangled skein, it is possible to find a certain peace.

Chapter One

I did not go to the Nude Beach much until after the old dogs died.
Their slow demise when they could no longer hike the wildlife
areas of the island had been excruciatingly painful for me. Worst
of all was having to play god with their lives—or more precisely,
with their deaths—having to say to my husband both times, well,
I guess today is the day we have to stop pretending we're letting
this go on for the dog.

I was bereft without dogs in the way that only those who
relate intensely to animals understand, which led me to contact
two Samoyed breeders—we always had Samoyeds. I was surprised by my reaction when the pups, only three weeks apart
in age, arrived. For months I often called them by the old dogs'
names, and I almost resented their presence. It wasn't until they
were almost a year old and I started taking them to the Nude
Beach at daybreak that I began to fully appreciate their lively
individual personalities. "Perhaps it was too soon," I admitted to
my husband, "but if they live their full span like the old dogs, I'll
be eighty by the time they're gone." If I'm lucky, I thought but did
not say aloud because my husband did not like such conversations. I still have one dog life left in my own years.

The Nude Beach was clear across the island from where we
lived, but I didn't mind that. The twenty-minute drive was beautiful, even in inclement weather, and I often felt like it was not
only the beginning of a new day, but the beginning of the world
as well. "Where were we when the foundations of the earth were

laid?" I would ask the dogs, an old Sunday-school memory surfacing imperfectly. "We were right here on Wapato Island, where
the first mists rose around us and the morning stars sang for joy."
Late autumn, when this story begins, the island crossing was the
loveliest of all, layers of blue fog skimming the meadows, ancient
oaks at the Marydell Dairy archeological site splitting the eastern sun, and Mount Hood mauve in the early morning light. I
drove slowly, not wanting to startle the bush birds into the car's
path. Doves rose from the hedgerows and California quail skit-
tered across the road; a small flock of geese, disturbed from their
feeding by a coyote slinking hopefully behind them in the field,
lifted in unison, and I lowered my window to hear their noisy
clatter.

Collins Beach was its official name, but no one I knew called
it that. Nude Beach, we all said. The paths leading through the
screen of cottonwoods to the sand were marked with signs that
read "Clothing Optional," except at the first path, where someone
had scribbled through the word *optional.* The locals who gathered in the mornings for coffee at the Reeder trailer park store
described it this way: "The first path is for families, the second is
for normal people who just like to take off their clothes, the next
for gay men, then one for lesbians, and another for transvestites."

"It's surprising how many old folks go there," said the clerk
when I stopped on the way home that morning for milk, "and
they hang out without a stitch, just like the kids." After I paid, the
clerk continued. "I don't care if people go around nude—not on
a nude beach, I mean. Let the naked truth hang out, that's what
I say. It all seems rather innocent to me. God brought us into the
world without clothes and to my mind that's the way we should
go out. Lewis and Clark considered the women's dress somewhat indecent when they stopped here 'cause the Indian women
wore only cedar-bark skirts in the warm weather—nothing on
top. That makes me laugh right out loud when I think about the
Nude Beach now and how crowded it is on sunny afternoons in
the summer, cars triple deep in the parking strip on weekends. I

can't help but wonder what Lewis and Clark would think about that."

Wappatoe is how Meriwether Lewis spelled the name of the potato-like tuber that provided the main article of trade for the natives of our island. On the map, though, they used Clark's spelling: Wapato Island. Most schoolchildren are aware that Lewis was a challenged speller, even by the standards of his time. What they are usually not told, however, is that Lewis committed suicide only a few years after the Corps of Discovery expedition ended. Not the sort of thing a teacher likes to present in a grade-school classroom about one of the American heroes of exploration. In this day of computer research, however, the fact is available even on Wikipedia, so any student who has picked Meriwether Lewis for the inevitable explorer biography probably knows about it.

In 1950, when I was in third grade, my absent father committed suicide, and even though I had no conscious memory of the man, his death, and especially the manner of it, affected me greatly. I didn't learn of Meriwether Lewis's suicide until I was in college, but I immediately latched onto the fact. I had become quite obsessed with the idea that my father had deliberately ended his life, and in my late twenties I set about fairly seriously to die, in an unfortunate chapter of my youth that I have explored in an earlier memoir. "Such is the unfortunate hold that a parent, especially one that isn't there, can have on a child's mind," said Eloise, an elderly cousin once removed who had known my father well. Eloise was right about that, not just for me, but for my brother as well, who repeated much of the pattern of our father's unhappy life. In the autumn of 2008 when my dreams began, my brother had been absent from my life for almost thirty years.

Like the clerk at the trailer park store, I didn't care whether people wore clothes, but I always wore mine on the Nude Beach, my lifelong body shyness heightened by age. If I came at first light, before the one law enforcement officer who was assigned to that part of the island was on duty, I could run my dogs the mile length of the beach and back again without their leashes. Clothing might be optional, but leashes were not, and tickets were at least a seventy-five dollar fine. During the long, rainy Oregon winter, however, when the ribald antics of naked sunbathers that drew the officer's presence were not in play, I could come in the afternoon as well, as did a few others with their unleashed dogs. Often some of the Odd Ones were there—the String-Can Man who tied bottles and cans together with fishing line and hung them high in trees, or the handsome bronze one I called Big Indian in my mind because of his long black hair and his penchant for going nude even in the coldest weather. Or the Builder, who was tall and professorial-looking with his slightly shaggy white hair. The Builder did not go nude, although if the sun was warm, he tied his shirt around his waist. He always acknowledged me by glancing sideways with a slight smile, not quite meeting my eyes but not avoiding me completely. He scoured the beach for planks or particularly straight poles of varying lengths and formed them into lean-to shelters with their open sides to the river. Once, when he was carefully dismantling a length of deck boards that had washed ashore, I stopped slightly below him on the sand and asked, "What are you building?"

He pointed downriver. "The wind comes," he said. "We have to be ready for the wind."

I had a dog now, Devi, who needed to run. Her name means goddess, but my husband Jim soon christened her The Devil Dog because she was so unpredictable. The other pup, Sherpani (Sherpa woman), Pani we called her, was much more like the Samoyeds we'd always had: playful, happy to be snooping in the flotsam or digging deep holes in the sand. With Pani the leash law would not have been a problem except to inhibit my own brisk pace. But for nervous Devi, who, with her narrow frame and long nose, looked more like a coyote than a Samoyed despite her registration papers, these early morning runs were a necessity. She fixated on gulls or cormorants flying above the water and raced them down the beach, yipping wildly, until she was a white speck in the distance. Always she returned, but it took successive runs before she settled into a normal dog routine. Why was I so indulgent of this dog's intense need to run? Was it that I had been a runner myself, had run my last marathon at sixty, had kept my own life on an even keel with occasional bursts of freedom, or at least the knowledge that had I needed to run, the freedom was there?

I kept a sort of diary I labeled the Nude Beach Notebook that consisted of my island walks, mostly on the Nude Beach, a record of both exterior and interior weather, observations of birds, and occasional historical information about the island I now called home. I included incidents from the popular histories and old explorer journals that captured my imagination, especially those of life that preceded the European occupation, sometimes scribbled elsewhere and later stuffed untidily in the notebook. Our moorage and the temporary nature of our floating homes seemed, to my somewhat romantic nature, almost a modern-day reincarnation of the native villages that in previous centuries had lined the river channel. After the dreams began, I wrote much about my brother and our shared childhood, and as the memories were rekindled, I became preoccupied with his unfortunate resemblance to our father. I wrote about it one day when I returned to the car after two miles on the beach.

I left the bed early while the old cold moon still bobbed in the river beside my upstairs study window. I have begun once more to dream about my brother, vague dreams that I do not quite remember when I come awake, only that the dream was about him or that he was standing somewhere in the background in a crowd of people. I did not leave the houseboat until a faint orange curve of light arced over the water and the newly arrived tundra swans across the channel in Burlington Bottoms rose in twinkling flocks beyond the skeleton of an old mill. Here on the Nude Beach some of the cottonwoods still cling fiercely to their last hint of color, flinging mottled coins in miserly handfuls. Last week late mushrooms lined the path from the road but now they are gone, perhaps eaten by deer. Neat pointed prints marched toward the water where whitened bones of beaver-skinned limbs lay scattered on the sand.

✑

We were talking about ghosts. The John Street Café in North Portland was our usual meeting place because it was quiet and had big windows, and the proprietor wore his hair in a long gray ponytail. Sometimes we talked about my writing and sometimes we talked about Madeline's. Occasionally we talked about death, as women our age tend to do. More often we talked about horses; both of us were crazy about horses. Someday we'd get one together, stable it on the island, and share the expense and care; it was a game we played. I had been reading Franz Boas's ethnographic study of the Chinook and how hard he had to look in 1890 to find one single speaker of the native language that had dominated the lower Columbia in its various dialects. I had just shared the Chinook legend about dying, which I'd paraphrased earlier in my notebook.

The late nineteenth-century anthropologist Franz Boas had located a man named Charles Cultee who still knew the old language and the customs that were followed on the lower Columbia River and this is what the old man said. When a person died a complex exchange took place between the dying person, the ghosts—the souls of the previously deceased—and the "seers" or shamans. All of these personages traveled in canoes. When a person was dying and the seers intervened, they paddled as far as the morning star to try to retrieve the soul. Sometimes they were successful and the ghosts, usually unwillingly, relinquished the soul and the person recovered health, even if he or she was previously considered dead. But if the soul had been fed by the ghosts or drunk of the water, it was too late and the person remained dead. On the lower Columbia River islands the bodies were placed in burial canoes and the spring floods carried them to the Pacific.

"I have a friend," said Madeline, "who saw a ghost, and I've heard her tell the story several times." It was a curious story indeed, for it initially involved only half of a ghost. Toward evening Laura had been walking along a road near Davis, California, when, a short distance in front of her, an apparition emerged from behind a pole. This apparition was the bottom half of a woman's figure, fully clothed in no particular period dress, walking at approximately Laura's pace. Startled, she stared hard at this partial person and began walking a little faster to catch up, but she made no discernible gain. Gradually the top half of the woman filled in. Suddenly, as mysteriously as the ghostlike figure had appeared, it began to fade, the top half first, and then it disappeared altogether. Laura went straight home and breathlessly reported what she'd seen to her husband, who was unimpressed, even somewhat dismissive, thinking at first she wasn't serious. Perhaps, he said, the woman ducked down in the ditch that was along the road. No, Laura insisted, she had that thought too and had looked carefully in the ditch for any sign that someone had passed, but there was none. "Her husband just flat-out didn't believe that she had really seen a ghost," concluded Madeline.

"Why was she so sure it was a ghost and not some trick her eyes were playing?"

"She is primarily a science fiction writer who grounds her stories in fact so she would have preferred to think this was a trick, but she knows what she saw," insisted Madeline.

"Do you believe her? You don't believe in ghosts."

"No, I don't believe in ghosts, but she simply wouldn't invent this story when it is so contrary to what she believes herself."

"I don't *believe* in ghosts either, but I do believe in unexplained coincidences. I've had some strange experiences here on the island that I can't explain logically at all, like the women at Black Ash Alley. That was a ghost kind of thing." The man with the ponytail brought our sandwiches while I told Madeline the story.

Black Ash Alley was what I called the strip of land between Mud and Sturgeon lakes because of the charcoal silhouettes the Oregon ash trunks made against the sunset glare. In the early autumn evenings this was a beautiful and mysterious place, even without ghosts. I had parked at the handicapped fishing ramp at Big Eddy on the Gilbert River and headed back toward the lakes through a swale of ash trees. I usually did this walk several times in the fall before Fish and Wildlife closed the area to everyone but hunters, taking note of the time of the sunset, watching for new snow on Mount Hood to the east, and recording in my notebook what day the migrating birds first appeared. During late August shorebirds like yellowlegs and faded avocets begin to show and by mid-September flocks of sandhill cranes arrive. Once I counted a flock of seventy-four white egrets, mostly standing in the trees.

The strip of land on which I was walking surely was a harvest camp for native women digging wapato. Lewis and Clark had described a large cache of short harvest canoes that were used for gathering the edible plant from the shallow lakes. The women, immersed to their armpits, walked beside the little boats while they felt in the mud for the small potato-like bulbs, which they loosened with their toes.

"I was thinking of that—thinking of the women in their cedar bark skirts, so of course I was set up for ghosts and what happened next," I admitted to Madeline.

The sun was extremely low, melting into Mud Lake, the trunks of the ash trees jet black against the golden light and perfectly still until the shadows started to move from one tree to the next, small black shapes about three or four feet high like children playing.

"It scared me, really. Then the shadows, for which I have no explanation whatsoever unless they were the result of my own aging eyesight, disappeared. At the same time, noises started, low guttural sibilant sounds that became more musical, as if water were bubbling or birds were talking, but I saw no birds."

It was too late in the season for the whispery sound of tree swallows. Whatever I had heard did not sound exactly like words, more like feminine whispers and laughter, feet on cool mud dancing, and sometimes sticks breaking. It wasn't loud. I scanned the trees all around, even across Mud Lake, with my binoculars, but I could detect no leaves moving and I saw no birds except two white egrets at the edge of the lake and a small flock of yellowlegs on the shore. The high tinkling cry of the yellowlegs could have accounted for the laughter sound, although the birds appeared to be feeding, not engaged in any conversation.

The sounds continued for a few minutes and then faded. So did the sun except for the blazing reflection of western clouds in the lake. I walked back to the car in the empty parking lot and finally the wind began. I could hear it in the trees—not like the sounds I had heard before but not totally unlike them either, and the amber light softened. "I was spooked," I admitted to Madeline, "but it was rather exciting, like I'd overheard something that hadn't been meant for me at all, like when you're a kid and hear adults say something they don't think you'll understand, but you do, and it adds a whole new dimension to a familiar situation."

"Did you tell Jim about this?"

"No. Jim would have reacted exactly the same way that Laura's husband did." Neither one of us spoke for a moment while a waitress, not the pony-tailed man, brought the bill. The John Street Café closed after lunch and that was probably a hint for us to leave. "So, Madeline," I asked, "what did your conference people say about the ghost? How did that play out?"

"Well, we tossed around different ideas for a bit and then I suggested one that seemed at least somewhat satisfactory. A lot of scientists now—physicists anyway—take quite seriously the idea of parallel universes. I asked Laura if she would be more inclined to accept an idea that had some basis in quantum physics instead of religion or superstition—that perhaps some membrane of a similar universe had momentarily intersected and that was what she had witnessed. She was somewhat receptive to that and said that she found the existence of parallel universes more credible than any conventional ghost concept."

"My ghosts were more like parallel time zones, some mixture of past and present that had to do with place."

"Some scientists consider that a possibility, too."

"Well, I'm not a scientist so I can't disprove or deny it. For me to *believe* in intersecting universes or time zones would require a leap of faith, something akin to believing in religion or ghosts. I remain an agnostic."

"So how did this Black Ash episode play out for you, then?"

"After I got home I read the rest of Boas's ethnographic study and his description of native language along the lower Columbia. He said that the language was extremely guttural and sibilant in comparison, say, to the Nez Perce, and that it had lots of onomatopoetic words. In fact, it was terribly complicated with sounds the Europeans didn't recognize as words; they recorded them derisively as grunts but in reality, in its varied dialects— maybe not so much the "jargon" trade form that developed—the language of the Chinook conveyed complex ideas like the sound of dancing, the wind, sticks breaking, or boiling water."

☙

The river was deep where we lived; almost forty feet during the high water of the late spring runoff, said the diver who did the float inspection when we bought the houseboat. Often when I focused on the way the wind skated here and there and changed the angle of the light, something bobbed up, maybe an otter or even a sea lion following the salmon in the spring. Under the surface lurked layers of life in the lower depths and layers of death as well, sometimes disturbingly close to the houseboats.

    The approach road to the moorage once ended at a ferry slip, which had been the main automobile access point for the island before the first bridge was finished in 1950. It still ran straight into the river on a ramp used by fishing and pleasure boats. The summer that we came, the ramp was redone as a more sophisticated boat launch and stolen cars that had been pushed into the water after joyrides had to be removed. First out, assisted by huge air bags that were inflated until they popped the car to the surface, was a Corvette, covered in brown and green slime. Next, a pick-up truck of no discernible color emerged from the murky depths. Then the diver bobbed up for a conference with authorities. In the remaining car the diver had spotted a body when he rubbed off some of the window muck.

    Everything slowed way down and the workers waited for the ambulance. How long had the body been there, anyway, just a few yards downstream from the end of the moorage and none who lived there had known? Two years, if this indeed was the car the authorities had identified with the license plate numbers from a missing person report. There should be two bodies, a woman and a child. The diver went down again and confirmed the suspicions. Two bodies—a woman and a baby. The ambulance went away, the police arrived, and a big flatbed truck backed down to the water line. Airbags were pumped full but the mud was loath to relinquish its treasure. It was spooky, all right, and sad, we moorage residents said to each other, even more so because of the baby, and we all went back to our houses because it was getting dark. Sometime in the night the car floated to the surface with a great sucking sound that no one at the moorage heard. It was loaded onto the flatbed truck and hauled away.

    The water stared back in a black motionless sheet when I leaned my forehead against the window in the upstairs study. Had the woman been lost and mistakenly driven into the river because of the poorly marked boat ramp? Or had she, in despair over a broken marriage and shattered future for her and the child, deliberately taken their lives? Slim currents of fog curled and uncurled above the water. I thought of the ongoing existence of souls and what I had once written about ghosts and seers in my notebook. The wind stirred and the fog tendrils began to organize into elongated shapes slightly above the water. I imagined a mud-covered Madonna with a child in her arms, freed from her metal prison, floating in a slim white fog canoe toward the sea.

❧

The Nude Beach did it—started the writing again, that is, and maybe the more frequent dreams, which I knew were about my brother but never could quite remember. At first I simply scribbled words in the sand, words that scattered when the dogs romped through them. Or Pani, thinking it was a game I was playing, grabbed the cottonwood branch I was using to write so I would throw the stick downstream at the edge of the water for her to retrieve. Sometimes I even wrote phrases on the beach; not poetry, really, not any definite syllabic form, or even any thought that would make sense to anyone but me. I wrote the words and phrases at the very edge of the water. The container ships headed for the ocean would make waves enough to erase them quickly, even if the tide was going out. They were not written for anyone who might come later in the day to read and wonder about, not for the Builder, carrying his smooth white poles and boards he had gleaned, or the Man with the Metal Detector, who said he had found three gold rings last year, one of them quite valuable.

The words I had written in the sand that day were names, first my brother's childhood name, Bobbie. His life had turned out badly, and I had not seen him in almost thirty years. The other word was our father's name, Robert. His life had turned out badly too, and I had often wondered whether some genetic factor this man had transmitted could have contributed to the misfortunes in my brother's life.

Perhaps it was just a coincidence that the very day I had uncharacteristically recorded the names I had written in the sand in my notebook, I heard a radio segment about brain research. A neuroscientist expounded on the relationship of a flattened orbital cortex and the amygdala, the area of the brain that controlled pleasure-seeking behaviors such as sex and abuse of chemically addictive substances. According to the expert being interviewed, a poorly functioning orbital cortex, the regulator of the amygdala in which those behaviors originated, was a serious genetic flaw; amoral, addictive, or even violent behavior could easily manifest, especially if the individual's abnormality had been exacerbated by childhood abuse. Perhaps my father had an abnormally flattened orbital cortex, I mused. Cousin Eloise, among others, had repeatedly described his behavior, even when outrageous by the community's Presbyterian standards, as "amoral." "It wasn't as if Robert didn't know right from wrong," Eloise said. "God knows, Uncle Arthur tried to beat it into him."

That was not news to me. Our father had been severely and repeatedly whipped as a child, I had been told several years earlier by his much younger brother, Howard. When I returned from the Nude Beach that morning I dug through files to find an old folder I had kept from previous family research with the notes from a phone conversation. Shortly after the phone call, I had written my uncle's very phrases into a sort of story. Was this fiction or nonfiction, I wondered now, rereading it, comparing the story to the notes I had taken? More importantly, I thought, was there any clue in our father's history as to why we had lost my brother? Neither Bobbie nor I had a conscious memory of this troubled man. Older neighbors and relatives had memories, though, and many had remarked on Bobbie's resemblance to our father in physical appearance and mannerisms. I smoothed the wrinkled paper; then, impulsively, I copied the short piece into my notebook. "Men in the Family: the Robert Factor," I wrote across the top of the page.

Howard could see his breath, a white balloon like the one for the words in the Katzenjammer Kids comic strip, but there were no words. Only a blank oval that formed and disappeared and re-formed each time he exhaled into the cold, moist air of the barn. Steam rose as the light crust of snow that had accumulated that afternoon on the cow's back melted, leaving black Brylcreem ringlets. Pulling the stool closer and placing a galvanized pail between his knees, Robert leaned his head against the sloping flank. Streams of milk pinged like plucked banjo strings until they drowned as the bucket filled. Then the sound was a different one, the same sound their father made after supper, sucking his tea through his teeth.

"Sing," Howard said, trying to fill the white balloon in front of his face. Robert often sang when he milked the cow, but tonight he did not seem to hear his youngest brother's request. Howard kicked his feet impatiently against the cement wall. Robert had set him on the ledge so the child would not get too close behind the cow. "Rob-ert," Howard insisted. They all called him Robert in the family, even after he died. He had been the first grandson, the boy named after his mater-nal grandfather Robert Clark, who was so pleased at the arrival of a boy that he wrote out a check for $1,000 and sent it to the new mother. "There will be a third generation of farmers," he purportedly said. "This money is to be used only to give him a start in farming."

"Sing," commanded the four-year-old Howard. Robert's face turned slightly, although all the boy could see was the outline of it and a shine on his older brother's cheek, a reflection from the light bulb above the cow. Could it be that Robert was crying, a big boy like him? Robert was the oldest of the four brothers, sixteen then, and Howard, only four, was the baby.

"Won't you sing?" Howard pleaded, his voice now with anxious tears in it, so Robert began, the same song he sang night after night about the goat that ate three shirts and the farmer who was so mad that he beat the goat hard with a stick and then tied him to the railroad track in hopes that the train would smash him to smithereens.

"Bill Grogan's goat," Robert sang.

"Bill Grogan's goat," Howard echoed.

"Was feelin' fine."

"Was feelin' fine."

"Ate three red shirts,"

"Ate three red shirts,"

"Right off the line."

"Right off the line."

But it was not Bill Grogan who had taken the stick and beaten the shirt-eating goat that afternoon, it was their father, and the stick had been used on Robert. Howard saw it from the bathroom window. The wooden shoe polish box on which the boy stood swayed slightly and he clenched his fingers fiercely over the sill. His eyes widened and he hiccupped as Robert leaned over the fence.

"Bill took a stick."

"Bill took a stick." Howard sang, but he was thinking of his father.

"Gave him a whack." Not just a whack—their father had beaten Robert, lick after lick with the supple whip until there were round red stains like cherries on the snow. Robert fell away from the fence. Their mother sobbed in the bedroom.

She had tried to stop the beating before it began. "He is too old to beat," she said to their father. "Some take longer to learn," he snapped back at her, grabbing the cherry switch from the corner. Robert, who was even taller than his father then, made no attempt to resist, but preceded him out the door. He took off his shirt even though the snow was already slashing across the field and he leaned over the top board of the fence. When their father came back in the house after the beating the parents did not speak but frozen words rose in white balloons between them.

The pail was full. A sweet bovine smell rose from the warm, foamy milk to mix with the sour scent of the darkened barn. Robert did not move his forehead from the cow's flank at first but finished the song about the goat tied to the railroad track by the angry farmer. In Howard's mind the farmer looked like his father with bib overalls and a denim coat that had a collar of corduroy. He wore a brown hat and his hand, in which he gripped the stick, had ribbed nails with dirt under them.

"The whistle blew." Robert sang softly now, his voice like chimes on the church organ.

"The whistle blew," Howard chimed softly, too.

"The train drew nigh."

"The train drew nigh."

"Bill Grogan's goat,"

"Bill Grogan's goat,"

"Was doomed to die."

"Was doomed to die."

That night after he'd put hay in the manger for the cow, Robert lifted the boy down from the wall. He carried the lantern and the pail of milk so there was no extra hand for Howard. "I'd carry you on my back," he said, "so as not to get snow in your shoes, but my back is sore tonight." Howard pictured the switch slicing into the flesh again and again with all the strength of their father's fury and the drops of blood on the snow. "I'll take small steps," Robert said, "and you can put your feet where I do." So Howard held the back of his brother's coat and put his shoes in the tracks that Robert had made.

Fiction or nonfiction? I'd have to ask Madeline about this, I decided. If one wrote in fiction to ferret out the truth of a situation, into what genre did the writing fall?

Facts from Uncle Howard's account:

The whipping

The supple switch

Blood like cherries on the snow

The $1,000 for the first grandson

The wooden shoebox in the bathroom on which Howard stood

The cement half-wall in the barn where Howard sat

Bill Grogan's Goat, which Howard sang in quavering voice

The shortened steps Robert took for Howard

Embellishments:

Steam from cow (from own childhood)

Sound of milk in pail (see above)

Ice-block conversation (paternal grandparents cold people)

When Uncle Howard told me this story, he was already blind. And now, fifteen years later, I could not ask him if my rendition of it was factual enough to qualify as truth, because he was dead.

Whether the story was true or not probably would not matter to my father.

"He lied," my baffled mother, who continued to love him until he died, said sadly, "when it would have been easier and more convenient to tell the truth" (*Prairie Reunion,* 192).

Could it be that his "lies" were like the embellished versions of events or circumstances that my brother began to use in adolescence, a vision of the world as he wanted it to be, not as it really was?

The next morning at the Nude Beach the fog hung low over the Columbia with an odd clear layer of silver light just above the water. About this time in early November 1805, the Corps of Discovery canoes had passed our island on their way downstream. Only a few years later Meriwether Lewis had committed suicide like my father. A theory among Lewis's relatives was that his death was murder, not suicide, but the accepted version was that Lewis, a heavy drinker with tangled finances, blew his head to smithereens with a gun. Years ago I read a speculation that he was bipolar and that once the Corps of Discovery expedition was completed, his behavior illustrated that he was suffering from deep depression.

My father didn't use a gun, or so the coroner's report said, anyway. He hooked up a hose to the exhaust pipe of the car. Persistent descendants of Lewis, wanting to settle the suicide question, petitioned to have his body exhumed, but permission to do so was denied by the National Park Service. What does it matter whether you dig them up or not? I wondered. There are other ways of resurrecting the dead.

✑

"Men in the Family?" asked Madeline the next day at the John Street Café. "About your missing brother?" She was delighted that I had finally started writing again after vowing to retire from what I called a difficult and thankless art. "This is an odd coincidence," she continued. "I have a brother, too, who has been absent from the family for nearly thirty years. Sometime in the early eighties was the last we heard of him."

"I didn't even know you had a brother. I've known you for over a decade, and you've never mentioned him."

"Why would I mention him? You don't talk about your brother, either. What's there to say when you're not even sure whether they are dead or alive?" I was pretty sure Bobbie wasn't dead. I'd been in occasional contact with his ex-wife Karen, who would know if he died and would have told me. Madeline was more interested in discussing writing than brothers. "But you wrote about your father, not your brother?"

I recounted the radio segment, the flattened orbital cortex that could be a genetic condition, and the potential consequences. "Actually," I confessed, "the man was researching mass murderers, hardly a category that fits either my brother or my father."

"But this story about your father's abuse—it's true?"

"It's close to the truth, I'm sure of that. Does that make it fiction or nonfiction?"

"You can write the truth in fiction; sometimes it's even more effective that way." The salads came, and Madeline put all her cucumbers on my plate. "Let's figure this out for you." Madeline was practical and efficient and wanted me to focus my energy. "Give me a one-sentence summary of what you're trying to do."

I couldn't do that, and it embarrassed me. I was just scribbling in the sand at the Nude Beach and stuffing papers in an untidy notebook. I should have waited until I could better explain myself before talking about what I had written. "Maybe I will have to find my brother before I do anything," I said rather lamely. Then I switched the conversation to horses and Madeline was happy to oblige. Neither of us wanted to talk about finding or not finding our brothers. In late summer we had been to the Youth and Yearling Challenge at the county fairgrounds, where twenty young girls competed to show their training skills in natural horsemanship, a method that emphasized gentleness and trust. Each girl had been given ninety days to work with a yearling mustang that had been culled from the wild herds. At the end of the competition some of the girls kept their yearlings and others offered them at auction to support the program. We discussed the feasibility of buying mustangs.

"What these girls have done is no small feat," said Madeline. "We should think about buying a yearling, one that has already been started in training. Some of them sell for less than a hundred dollars." So we thought about that: thinking about horses was easier than thinking about brothers who were lost.

"I know a horse that's thirty-two years old," I said, "and if we got a yearling . . . it wouldn't be fair to the horse. No way does either of us have thirty years of active horse care left." When did we start talking this way, measuring our decisions on remaining lifespan? It wasn't until we were walking to our cars that we resumed the talk of absent family members.

"Was your brother Bobbie abused, too?" Madeline was trying to help me connect my thoughts, trying to train my wild mustang musings into more disciplined paces. Natural writership, like the natural horsemanship that was so in vogue, I thought with some amusement. I appreciated her tenacity, her gentleness and trust.

"No, certainly he wasn't abused in any physical way. But he was abandoned. I guess that could be considered a form of abuse. All of us were abandoned." Yes, *all* of us, I thought, as I watched

Madeline drive away. I did not start my car immediately; instead I wrote for some time in my notebook.

Once in summer when I was about eight or nine and standing in the Scotch Grove Presbyterian Church basement that smelled musty because the dehumidifier had quit, a girl with dark brown hair like mine came running up to me. "You're my sister, you're my sister," the little girl said, but I was so surprised at the unexpected greeting that I did not answer at all, and the brown-haired girl ran back to wherever she had come from.

On the short drive home our mother, who had ended up with our three half-sisters in her Sunday school class, said this: "They were visiting their grandfather, and he brought them to church with him. They are your father's children with Dorothy, but he has left them, too." Then she stopped the car on the gravel road and turned to make sure that both of us would hear her clearly. "Bobbie, Barbara, listen to me. Those three little girls were left in an orphanage. You must never, ever blame them. You were all just children."

⌀

Again I had awakened too early, but this time the person in my dream was a woman with short brown hair. I knew for sure where this dream had come from, and before I slipped carefully out of bed so as to not awaken my husband, I recreated the exact scenario in my head, not of the dream but of the incident that triggered it. Once in my study I recorded this continuation of yesterday's memory carefully into my notebook.

When my research for the family memoir was complete and as much as I could put together of an old puzzle with lost pieces twisted into an acceptable story with beginning, middle, and end, I stood on the southern porch of the Iowa farmhouse where I had lived as a child. A lectern borrowed from the Scotch Grove Presbyterian Church had been placed for my reading. The sun stabbed my eyes when the wind shifted the elm leaves and blotted out the individual faces in a considerable crowd of people, a crowd that seemed it must include everyone I had ever known in my childhood, even those who had already died, milling about on the lawn.

Into the early morning hours I had battled a migraine headache that brought me to my knees. I had literally crawled from what my grandmother had always called the hired man's room, even though there had never been a hired man in my memory, to the bathroom that had been remodeled by my cousin Vaneta. She owned the ancestral farmhouse now and ran it as a bed and breakfast called Sweet Memories. I vomited three times into the toilet, and thank god everything disappeared when I pulled the chain. All during my childhood a bucket of water had stood on a newspaper beside this stubborn piece of porcelain to assist its flush. It was used only for nighttime pees. Anything else, if it was snowing too hard to go to the outhouse, my grandmother reminded me daily, must be deposited in the chamber pot in the corner and emptied promptly the next morning into the swill pail to be taken behind the chicken house and sloshed out with old apple cores and potato peelings.

Using only the nightlight on the stairs, I groped my way to the kitchen, where I fixed a cup of coffee. Caffeine usually helped at this stage when my body felt emptied of whatever toxic substance had precipitated the headache, and that night the coffee did not fail me. Gratefully, I held the cup against first one temple and then the other. Finally the pain subsided almost entirely except for a small intermittent stab behind my left eye, and I returned to the hired man's room where I slept for an hour.

The only reminder by afternoon of the headache was the nimbus effect that formed over any object on which I solidly fixed my gaze. This made the relatives, all the people from the church and those who had once been neighbors, appear to be angels, perhaps people who had died in my long absence and returned now to Earth to hear how I presented their lives in a book. This reading at the farmhouse was a cockamamy scheme hatched by someone from the New York publisher's office, I thought wearily, the sleepless hours I had lost to the headache hitting me suddenly. The venue was the most painful for me that they could have chosen to launch this book. Perhaps the plan had been made with the bookseller from Iowa City, who had set up a table on the lawn in front of the old-fashioned rose bush and was selling a book to everyone in sight. The hardest part was being asked the same question again and again about my brother.

"So nice to see you again, Barbara. Why did you stay away so long? Have you any news of your brother? Your mother was so proud of Bobbie when he was in the army that it seems such a shame, the way things turned out. We have all been so worried about him." I simply shook my head in response to their questions, as I had not heard from my brother in several years.

After the reading, which had gone tolerably well in spite of the sun in my eyes, the bookseller seated me at a table and politely asked the people in line to write their names on a piece of paper as well as what inscription they would like in their books. That was considerate, I thought in relief, for how would I ever call each one's name to mind when they had all aged thirty-five years and looked more like their parents whom I had known in my childhood than any memory I had of the faces immediately before me. I met everyone's eyes, smiled and exchanged pleasantries as I signed the copies of the book. At least four times someone remarked on my white hair. "I always think of you in braids, Barbie," a neighbor said, "riding your horse across the field with those long dark braids bouncing on your back."

It was after the fourth time that remark was made that I again saw the small brown-haired woman standing on the fringe of the crowd. I had noticed her during the reading and had almost lost my place in the narrative. I know who that is, I thought with part of my mind, even though I had only met her once several decades ago when we were both still children. What kind of egomaniac was the man anyway, I thought, to name his son after him and later a daughter, too? When the line had finally diminished and only a straggler now and then came over to pick up a second copy of the book for yet another relative or neighbor who had moved away, I left my chair and worked my way through the crowd to the woman who had caught my attention. Our eyes locked as I approached. She somewhat resembled me, although she was shorter with dark hair. Perhaps it is dyed, I thought, for she is only a few years younger than I am. I held out my hand, more to ward off than to welcome her. She leaned toward me, trembling, with tears streaming down her face. "You are Roberta," I said.

"I feel like I should apologize for my mother." The dark-haired woman's voice was barely audible, and for a few seconds her body held perfectly still. Nearby people turned to stare at her, for she was not someone who was known in the community, and her trembling began again. "Yes, I'm Roberta," the woman whispered. "They call me Bobby."

Of course, I thought. We called my brother Bobbie, too. This is Dorothy's daughter, the second one. Putting one arm around her, a gesture more obligatory than heartfelt, I said softly, "No apology is necessary, least of all by you. We were all children."

So it was back to the Nude Beach as soon as the light came down the river. A heavily loaded container ship was moving downstream on the outgoing tide. *Hanjun* was printed on its side, and the waves in its wake curled like rolling surf on a crescent of ocean beach. Devi was wild with delight and plunged again and again into the foam, while Pani, timid about getting even her feet wet and worried about her more adventurous sister, stood on drier sand and barked. When Devi emerged from the waves, Pani grabbed her tail in her teeth and tried to slow her down.

That day when I wrote *Bobbie* in the sand and, farther down, wrote *Robert*, it was not only my brother who came to mind. It had been over forty years since our mother had died of a sudden heart attack. The flat, white half-moon still hung in the west, thinned by the brimming daylight. *Half-sisters*, I wrote in the notebook. I had to think to remember their names.

Billie Mae, Roberta, Betty Jean.
We were all just children.

◯

This had become a morning ritual, the walk on the Nude Beach and the writing in the sand. When the dogs raced through my brother's name, I moved higher on the slight slant of the beach and wrote it again, and then I wrote Robert beside it. No one in the rural Iowa community in which we had lived as children had ever called my brother Robert, but I left both names there anyway. Your brother, he looked so much like your dad, our neighbor Paul Ernie told me after my brother had disappeared and I was back in Iowa for research, acted like him, too, even talked like him, sweet with the women and so easy with money.

How did Bobbie even copy our father's mannerisms, I wondered, when we were no more than babies when he left and we never saw him again? The names I had written in the sand would disappear by the next day, erased by the tide or the rain or the container ships with their rolling wakes, and I would write them again. In the notebook I wrote only descriptions of nature, the ducks I had seen on the ponds or the ragged skeins of hysterical fowl that circled above me on the beach when the guns were booming in the fields. I amused myself by copying the language and odd spelling of old journals. "A Cloudy morning Som rain ... Swans, Geese, ... & Sand hill Crane, they were emensely numerous and their noise horrid" (The Journals of the Lewis & Clark Expedition, Clark, November 5, 1805).

I needed focus: a one-sentence summary of what I was trying to do, like Madeline said, but I could only write names in the sand. What *was* I trying to do? In all honesty, I said to myself as I threaded through the tangled snares of willow roots while the dogs frolicked, I was not trying to find my brother.

Not too long after my brother dropped out of sight, I had been plagued by vague dreams of him like those that were haunting me now, so I contacted the Salvation Army and set up a missing person file. "We'll try to help," the kind lady said, "but we can only give out information with the person's consent." Was he sleeping somewhere on the street because of the drinking? Perhaps he was dead, and I didn't even know. No, I'd surely know that, I repeated firmly to myself, I would have felt it when he died. We had been so close in childhood that even our family called us twins. Our mother died when I was in college, and Bobbie was in the army in England. After that we grew apart, both physically and mentally, not wanting to confess our marriage failures to each other.

Finally, a card came from Karen, my ex-sister-in-law, with a Florida phone number. "Just in case," it read. "He always talked so much of you." So she knew where he was, but I was embarrassed to call her because of his drinking. I called the Salvation Army instead to close the file. I did not want to waste their meager resources now that I had a way to contact him. "Why, thank you," said the kind woman, when I said I would send them fifty dollars with my next paycheck. "You don't need to do that, you know. We've just put his name on a list and that list only gets longer; so many families lose track of their alcoholic relatives. You're lucky to have found him—we seldom get calls like this." I didn't confess I hadn't called the number I had been given, just filed the card in my address book. What could I do if I found him, I asked myself. Our conversations had mostly involved elaborate fantasy games to avoid painful realities, even when we were close as children. Besides, I told myself defensively, I had struggles in my own life, two sons for whom I was mostly responsible, and my teacher's salary barely covered expenses. What did you say to an alcoholic brother? Perhaps he didn't want to be found.

That didn't stop the relatives, especially Eloise and my cousin Vaneta, with whom I stayed in the ancestral farmhouse when researching family mysteries in the early nineties. With each contact, Bobbie popped up in the conversation. That day when I went back to the houseboat, I didn't write anything new in the Nude Beach Notebook. Instead, I reread and copied lines from what I had written years earlier, trying to understand myself why, even now, I did not want to actively search for my brother.

Vaneta looked at me steadily. "Have you tried to help him?" With difficulty I pulled my focus to the conversation of the moment.

"Vaneta," I said with a touch of exasperation, "just because his biological composition is a little more traceable to me than to other human beings doesn't mean he owes me any explanations. He has a right not to be found, if he chooses" (*Prairie Reunion*, 274-275).

It was oddly comforting to reread those lines, which made it seem as if I had refrained from contact for my brother's sake as well as my own. I knew that he was in ill health now, in some sort of nursing home, according to Karen, with whom I had finally gotten in touch, yet I still did not seek him out, even though the dreams persisted. Obviously I was shirking familial responsibilities by this stage of the game, and I had no excuses to offer, even to myself. I tried to quit thinking about it and for some weeks I refrained from writing the names in the sand. When I met Madeline at the John Street Café we discussed anything but missing brothers—her writing instead of mine, or horses, scheming toward what seemed at our age an alarmingly truncated future. I read books instead of even trying to write, books I had purchased for other projects, mostly abandoned, island histories or online journals from early explorers who had passed Wapato Island. What did it matter whether I wrote my brother's name in the sand or not, I told myself. It was winter now. Almost every day the rains came and in Oregon, sooner or later, the rains would erase almost anything.

❧

And then there was Eloise. For inducing guilt, Eloise made Vaneta look like a piker. In my childhood I had not even thought of my father's first cousin as a relative; that whole side of my parentage was a blank page on which connections would be drawn later. I'm not sure I even knew then that my paternal grandmother, who lived in Minnesota, and Eloise's mother were sisters, and I certainly didn't know how much Eloise had loved my father. What Eloise represented in my mind was the Scotch Grove Presbyterian Church. The church, however, was not a blank page. The church, that white diminutive building that had been originally established in 1847 by Eloise's Scottish ancestors, a mile and a half down the barely graveled road at the edge of my grandfather's land, stood tall in my mind, with good reason. Until I left for college, I had attended service there "every Sunday of my life," or so it seemed to me when I wrote about it later.

So Eloise *Sutherland* Helgens was my cousin-once-removed because her mother and my father's mother were Clarks, which somehow made me a Clark, too, a fact that had not yet registered when I listened during the church service for Eloise's lovely alto, which carried the whole congregation in song. And because she was the last living descendant of the original Sutherland founders—who made their difficult way from the Scottish Highlands to the Red River Settlement in Manitoba and twenty years later came in oxcarts down the Red River Trail to Iowa—Eloise became the first woman elder in a church not famous for its enlightened attitudes toward women. In fact, even my German grandmother was mildly scandalized. "Oh, for heaven's sake," said my mother, a shy woman who usually did not contradict my grandmother. "Eloise is surely smarter than all the men." Eloise had a four-year college degree and had served in the woman's auxiliary to the Marine Corps during the Second World War.

I had re-established our connection when I was researching my family memoir, and Eloise, a voracious reader, had taken an interest in my writing. She was a valuable resource for information about my father, full of stories that I was destined to hear repetitively, mostly of their childhood when her family went to Minnesota for their annual Independence Day vacation. Often these stories ended with a remark that made me singularly uncomfortable: "You'll redeem Robert yet," she would always say. "You're like him in so many ways—the good parts, I mean." That would be followed by the inevitable lecture about my duty to go and find my brother.

On an afternoon in mid-March when the sun unexpectedly broke through the clouds, I decided to return to the Nude Beach for a second dog walk. The trails in Forest Park where I often went in the afternoon would be slick, and the trees would drip incessantly in the aftermath of the heavy shower. I was feeling somewhat discombobulated because Eloise, who now lived in a retirement community in Mesa, Arizona, had called and requested my presence.

"I want you to come to Mesa, Barbara. There are some things that I need to attend to before I die."

"Are you feeling ill, Eloise?" Eloise's demands for visits were becoming more frequent and much as I enjoyed the camaraderie that had developed between us in the past few years, the trips to Mesa were inconvenient and they left Jim responsible for the dogs. He did not take them to the Nude Beach, and by the time I returned from Mesa, the ever-restless Devi had always ravaged a pillow or a rug.

"My health is beside the point, Barbara. When you are over ninety you are always ill with something and you simply choose what to complain about. You said you would come if I needed you, and I will pay for the ticket."

"I don't want your money, Eloise." Eloise's money got in the way of all sorts of things.

"You make it hard to be friends with you, Eloise," I had once said, "because you have too much money."

"You needn't worry I'll waste it on any of my profligate relatives," Eloise replied tartly. "You included. Anyone who takes perfectly good corn land that her grandfather drained and earlier relatives wrested from the wilderness and turns it back to tall grass prairie has no need of money from me." I had done that with the farmland I inherited, and Eloise had never ceased to complain about it. But several times, now, money had come for the airline tickets, and I knew it would come again. That made Eloise's commands hard to refuse, so I had scheduled the trip.

The dogs, barking wildly in anticipation of this second unleashed run, barked all the way across the island as I drove to the Nude Beach that afternoon. In a field along the road a flock of snow geese behind the snowberry hedgerow rippled and rose, then settled again. Before long they would leave for their summer breeding ground on Russia's Wrangle Island. Perhaps some of the Odd Ones would be at the beach this afternoon; they always appeared with the sun. Where they came from or how they got there with the first break in the clouds I did not know. Our island was over ten miles from Portland.

Sure enough, just beyond the entrance for normal-people-who-just-like-to-take-off-their-clothes, the String-Can Man was already hoisting a new collection of cans and bottles high into a cottonwood with a skinny branch. Both the dogs and I let him pursue his task without any obvious notice, as he never wanted to meet our eyes. A few other people, all fully clothed except for a young girl who carried her shoes, had come to the beach as well. A golden retriever puppy that seemed to belong to the girl with the red bare feet jumped up and licked my face.

I was feeling resentment over the impending trip to Arizona. I had finally started writing the names in the sand again. My brother Bobbie had been a favorite of Eloise and there would be questions and the usual admonitions about how I should be actively trying to find Bobbie. "Whatever would your mother say?" Eloise would ask. "You know she would want you to help your brother." "I don't know if he wants to be found, Eloise," I would reply, my usual excuse. "Maybe one whose life has turned out badly has a right not to be found."

Just below the curve where the willow shoots grew almost to the river, the Builder was carrying a board that had washed ashore, and the dogs ran up to him, wagging their tails in recognition. He faced me squarely as I passed lower on the beach and regarded me without embarrassment. For the first time he actually met my eyes and perhaps it was my imagination, but I thought he smiled slightly, so I waved. If I found my brother would he look like that—tall, white hair like my own, a rumpled but fairly clean sweatshirt? I saw the Builder here almost every afternoon I came. What was his story? Had he sacrificed a promising career to alcohol? Did he once have a family, a wife or parents who wanted to be proud? Although he smiled when he saw me now and greeted the dogs warmly, I would never ask him questions like that. Just by looking, I could tell he was a man who did not want to talk about his past. In fact, he spoke only of the wind when he spoke at all.

"Quite the artful beach house you're building there," I called.

He regarded me seriously. "The wind will shift," he said, pointing north. He had lined this newest lean-to with boards and limbs in a double layer on the downstream side. "The wind." He repeated his familiar line and his white hair lifted slightly as he faced downstream. "We have to be ready for the wind."

The wind wasn't bothering me this afternoon, but the upcoming trip to Arizona and another potential confrontation with Eloise about Bobbie and familial responsibilities was. At least this time I had new information for her, culled from the reading I'd been doing in the past few months while I wasn't writing. Not about my brother, of course, but something that related to the other common denominator in our relationship: the Scotch Grove Presbyterian Church. I had written it out carefully, hoping to deflect her interest when she began the familiar harangue.

Reminder: Be sure to tell Eloise of the surprising link I've just found between the Scotch Grove Presbyterian Church her Sutherland ancestors founded in Iowa and the Chinook natives of the lower Columbia in Jean Murray Cole's *Exile in the Wilderness,* the biography of Archibald McDonald.

A) In 1813 Archibald McDonald of the Hudson's Bay Company guided a group of Scottish peasants who had been displaced in the

Highland Clearances to the Red River Settlement (now Winnipeg).
Among them, Eloise's ancestors, John Sutherland and his family,
as well as uncles and other kin. After twenty years in Canada, John
Sutherland's son (also John), came down the Red River trail with eight
sons in an oxcart train to claim land in Iowa and establish our church.

B) After this same Archibald McDonald, in spite of harrowing hard-
ships that included a snowshoe journey along the Hudson Bay for
several hundred miles with these peasants, had safely delivered them
to the Red River Settlement, he was sent west to Fort George (Astoria)
to inventory supplies and take charge of the stores. He remained for
the next season.

C) Chief Concomly, the "wealthiest and most influential" Chinook
chief on the coast, had his impressive village across the Columbia
River from Fort George. A shrewd trader with the Europeans, Concomly
was delighted when his beautiful daughter, the black-haired Raven,
caught the eye of Archibald McDonald.

D) According to Ranald McDonald, the only child of this union, who
later became a famous adventurer in the Orient, the princess bride and
her groom, in the custom of Chinook royalty, walked to the marriage
ceremony on "a path of golden sheen," an aisle among giant cedars
that had been covered with the fur of beaver and otter.

E) Princess Raven died within a year, soon after her son Ranald
was born. Archibald McDonald had insisted on her conversion to
Christianity and her name had been changed to Sunday.

❧

I loved Eloise and her inexhaustible supply of stories, no matter how many times I had heard them, but it was so warm in the
retirement home apartment that I envied my cousin, who came
frequently from Minnesota to help Eloise with her financial
affairs, who had fallen asleep on the couch. He snored slightly.

"When I was a child, Barbara, all the Iowa Clarks went to
Aunt Kitsy and Uncle Arthur's for the Fourth of July, and we

stayed together in that Green Lake summer cabin, The Dew Drop Inn. Robert and I were in a league by ourselves as the old-est ones with all the other younger cousins. We talked about things a lot, real things, I mean, and in spite of the infrequency of our contact, I probably knew your father, Barbara, better than anyone except his brother Harold." This was Eloise talking, and the Minnesota cousin, asleep on the apartment couch, was a son of the aforementioned Harold. "Harold always had some sort of excuse for his brother. I know both Harold and Howard felt their father was terribly mean to Robert, and I heard about the whip-pings from my mother. My mother and Aunt Kitsy were excep-tionally close, even for sisters.

"Aunt Kitsy's real name was Mary—of course you know that, Barbara, as she was your grandmother. Just like my mother's name was Margaret Blanche and everyone called her Blanche. My name is Mary Eloise but most people know me only by Elo-ise. Everyone in the Scotch Grove community and the church has always called me Eloise, but during the war when I was in the Marine Corps, I was Mary."

I could have recited this story to anyone in Eloise's voice. There are people we have loved and known so well that we can talk in their voices, and that's how close I became to Eloise near the end of her life. She made these ancestors come alive for me as she recounted their loves and grievances. How Grandfather Rob-ert Clark hadn't liked Uncle Arthur from the get-go; how he was furious when Aunt Kitsy and Uncle Arthur moved from Iowa to Minnesota, and how Eloise's mother was the go-between—the one who carried messages from Aunt Kitsy to her parents. How Blanche was the one who heard the stories about Robert, starting with the trauma of his birth and his poor little head, misshapen from the protracted labor, a red mark from the forceps they used to pull him out. He wore a big cap in the few baby pictures that were sent to Iowa. Whenever Aunt Kitsy wrote of Robert's trou-bles later, she included something about his difficult birth, as if somehow her narrow hips were responsible for his problems. Then Eloise would speak of the mark of Cain.

"I know my mother had a Biblical interpretation of Robert's strange behavior. She called that red spot the mark of Cain, and she mentioned it so many times that I looked for it carefully once when I was pretending just to comb Robert's hair. I never saw even a remnant of where it had been."

Next would be the digression about the check, the thousand-dollar check that the grandson Robert had been promised as the first male heir, a birth that mended my grandmother's riff with her father. And how Robert had never seen a lick of that money.

"Now, one thousand dollars doesn't sound like much today, but to a boy in those days it must have sounded like a million dollars, like those kids with trust funds. I think Robert grew up with the feeling that he would have been rich but his father cheated him out of it. It is my firm opinion that check caused all sorts of mischief.

"It is a sorry thing, Barbara," Eloise admonished me, her much younger first-cousin-once-removed who had become her favorite object of moral instruction, "to think there is endless money behind you to bail you out. Robert thought that, and it is evident that your brother Bobbie thought that, too, although his grand ideas probably came from all that land that your mother's family gained during the Depression." Stroking her chin, a repetitive habit that often resulted in another lapse while she hunted for the tweezers to pull out an errant white hair, Eloise returned to her story.

"In an odd way I suppose that summer when I was fourteen and he was sixteen I was a little in love with Robert, even though he was a cousin. He was handsome and so gentle with all of us, and teenagers don't have much control over their emotions. 'Why, Eloise,' he'd say, 'You're turning out to be so pretty.' That wasn't true; I was a big horse of a girl, not the kind boys paid much attention to, but I wanted to believe him. That summer Robert took me out several times in a little flat-bottomed rowboat they had at Green Lake."

This could have turned into the story of the time my father borrowed a plane (or stole it, Eloise said, for he had never flown a plane in his life) and flew home from Minneapolis to the farm, taking the neighbor girl with him. (I think he got it somehow from those gangsters he was riding shotgun for on those liquor runs from Chicago during Prohibition, the Minnesota cousin, when he was awake, would say, adding his two bits of family lore.) Or it could have been the story about how they were all so amazed when Robert talked his new father-in-law, the stingy old Gid Hughes, into loaning him the money to take my mother, Kate, to Florida for a honeymoon. But today it would be the Green Lake story.

"Now Green Lake was a wide shallow lake and the sand was just as pure and white underneath the water. One sultry afternoon when all the little cousins were taking a nap and the parents were sitting in those old rusty metal chairs under the trees talking about old times, Robert, who could never sit still, you know, said he would row me across the lake. 'Don't go that far,' Uncle Arthur said. 'You stay where we can see you and watch the weather. You never know in this kind of heat when a thunderstorm might come up.' So Robert promised we would stay within sight of the shore, and we set off in the boat. I don't think even a cloud threatened, and there wasn't any wind."

Each time this story was told, more specific memories surfaced: the smell of the warm sun on the old wood and the soft feel of the damp boards across the bottom of the rowboat on bare feet; the metallic scrape of the oarlock; the soft slurp as the wooden oars came out of the water for each stroke; the nervous twinge Eloise felt when she realized the people in the lawn chairs and on the dock were so far away that they looked like sugar ants. The rowboat slowed to a stop.

"'Eloise,' Robert said in a dreamy sort of voice, 'Do you believe in God?' I was stunned at his question. Of course we all went to church and even though they were Methodists in Minnesota and we were Presbyterians in Iowa, we all certainly believed in God."

Eloise stroked her chin again and described the small ribbed waves that spread evenly a few feet from the boat before they drowned in the flat surface of the lake right before the odd cloud spread across the sky.

"'And do you really think that when we die that we go to heaven or hell?' Imagine your father asking me that!"

As if I could imagine my father at all, never having met him.

"'Of course,' I told Robert. 'Isn't that what the Bible says—that He shall come to judge the quick and the dead?'"

"'Well, I'm going to hell in a handcart already, that's what my father always says. He says I'm no son of his but a son of the Devil, and I'm doomed to die an awful death and go to hell.'"

Eloise was unsure what to say about that. "We weren't supposed to know about the beatings. What did I know about God? Just what we'd been told in the Scotch Grove Presbyterian Church, and that wasn't hopeful for Robert." Her mother had fretted about Robert's future every time a letter came from Aunt Kitsy. 'Robert's in trouble again, my mother would say before she even opened the envelope.' Then I'd hear the story again of his birth, the misshapen head and the red mark on his forehead when he was a baby."

That's when Eloise saw the reflection of the odd cloud, just before the first wind skated across the water. Eloise's mother told her that shortly after they had left in the rowboat, the radio music was interrupted by tornado warnings—twister clouds had been sighted coming up from the south. Her mother and Aunt Kitsy ran down to end of the dock and tried to call, but the little boat was already too far away for them to hear. The strange cloud, knobby like a big clenched fist, moved over the horizon and the mothers were immediately terrified.

"To this day," said Eloise, her voice tinged with old remorse, "I've felt guilty about my mother frantically running up and down the Green Lake shore, spraining her ankle on the rocks, screaming my name hysterically while the men carried all the blankets into the cabin to beat the rain. Your grandfather, Barbara, was angry rather than worried. 'I'll kill that boy,' he said. 'I've brought the switch.' I thought it odd even then that Uncle Arthur brought the switch to the lake in case he needed to whip Robert."

After the first sweep of wind that rocked the boat, the water grew flat and still and turned an ominous color. Robert stood right up in the flat bottom of the boat and dropped the oars. Luckily they stayed securely in the oarlocks, because Robert was oblivious to their fate as he stood there pointing at the cloud. It was huge and dark, and one curved tendril snaked out of it; then it straightened slightly like a large index finger.

"'It's pointing at me,' said Robert in a voice full of wonder, and he reached his hand toward the sky with his own finger extended. I tell you, Barbara, when Edwin and I went on that world tour with the Airstream club, and we saw the Sistine Chapel ceiling with the famous space between the fingers of God and Adam, I thought of that long-ago summer on the lake and the way that cloud leaned down in an almost human way. 'Eloise, look,' Robert shouted. 'It's pointing right at me; do you know what that means?'"

The little boat spun around like a leaf on top of the water. Eloise knew what it meant, all right. It meant this was a tornado, that she would never see her mother again and be able to apologize for going out so far on the lake.

"It meant both Robert and I were doomed to die."

How odd that as Eloise got more and more worked up telling this story, I fought off sleep in the hot apartment, thinking of my Uncle Howard's song about the goat tied to the railroad track.

Eloise sat back in her chair with force, clapped her hands once as she was wont to do when excited, and her sore, crooked feet bounced on the hassock so hard that it bounced, too. The Minnesota cousin on the couch woke up with a start, and the woman in the retirement apartment below heard that thump and thumped back with the broom handle on the ceiling, the way she did when Eloise had the TV on too loud because she couldn't find her hearing aids.

"But I was wrong," continued Eloise. "God intervened and we didn't die. As suddenly as it had appeared, the green cloud veered toward the northeast, and we were left with hardly any rain and only an ordinary wind, not one blowing in circles. It was a miracle. The worst force of the storm had quite entirely passed us by. We heard later that a twister touched down near Spicer, but no one was killed, just a barn destroyed and a cow or two thrown up in the air. When we finally reached the dock, I ran for my mother. Both she and I were still crying in fright, and Robert was led away. None of us, least of all Robert, ever said a word about it, but we knew he was soundly whipped for taking me out on the lake."

❦

Now to try to unravel the mixed emotions a visit to Eloise always engendered. Thank god for the Nude Beach. I was glad to be back in Oregon, which seemed so soft and green after the harsh desert world of Arizona, glad for the excuse to walk by the river to exercise the dogs. The snow geese were gone from the field so birds were on the move all right, and as I got out of the car, I noted four white pelicans in the shallow temporary lake that had formed in the meadow. Now that was odd—the pelicans usually hung out on Big Sturgeon, and in the autumn I saw them over on Steelman Lake. Pelican, I wrote in the sand.

I couldn't have been more than eight or so when I found a card postmarked Orlando, Florida, in the carnival glass bowl collection of old valentines and Christmas greetings. Our mother had said that they never should have taken a trip they couldn't afford and that she regretted to that day that they hadn't been able to repay her father the borrowed money before he died. The card had a cartoon version of a pelican on the front, a palm tree, a scantily clad woman with oversized breasts, and a sing-song verse. *A funny old bird is a pelican; his beak can hold more than his belly can; food for a week he can hold in his beak; and I don't know how in the hell-he-can. Greetings to Gid and Dena, Wish you were here, Bob and Kate.*

The handwriting belonged to our father. Bobbie and I thought the verse delightfully wicked as we were not allowed to swear, but the card disappeared, and I could never find it again. After my father's death, our grandmother Kitsy asked our mother to come to Minnesota so she could know something of Robert's children. While there I found a large pink shell on a shelf in the bedroom. I asked my paternal grandmother where it came from. "Florida. It came from Florida, Barbara," my grandmother Kitsy said in a thin voice. "Or maybe it came from Hawaii. At any rate, your father brought it."

The drenched beach gleamed and the flat water tilted ever so slightly, a calm lake now at slack tide, seemingly without current, yet a log not far from shore moved downstream at an alarming rate. The Columbia here was a large, inscrutable river much wider and more powerful than the channel of the Willamette that ran under our houseboat before it joined the big river at the end of the island. My walk past both wing dams that stretched out in the water was uneventful except for the antics of the dogs, which I barely noted in their familiarity, and I was grateful for the solitude. Near the downstream end of my walk, I had a surprise encounter on the usually empty early-morning Nude Beach.

This morning I saw the Man-with-the-Camera. This is the second time I have seen him sitting in the Blue House, but I did not speak that first time and neither did he. The Blue House is what I call the largest lean-to, probably one the Builder has made, because it has been, for some time now, covered with a blue tarp. I was surprised to see the man as I had come especially early, and the weather was not conducive to photos. The golden lip that had momentarily crested the cloud line as the sun came up had already disappeared. "Good morning," I said tentatively, noting the camera he had set up on a tripod. Maybe he wanted pictures of birds, and I should tell him that the main flyway from Ridgefield Wildlife Refuge across the river seemed to be a little farther upstream, near the entrance for normal-people-who–just-like-to-take-off-their-clothes. "Are you a wildlife photographer?"

He had a blanket wrapped around him as there was a chilly wind, and the clouds that earlier let through shafts of light had hardened. "I'm hoping for red in the sunrise," he answered, and he looked away at the gray sky above the Washington shore. I walked the short distance remaining to the sign that read "End of the Nude Beach" in hand-painted letters. When I passed him on my return, I spoke again. "No red today," I said. "That's a cold wind—I hope you have coffee." His look softened as if he was surprised that I was at all concerned about his comfort. He held up a thermos with an ungloved hand. "I have coffee," he replied with a slight smile. Another one of the Odd Ones, I thought. Then he raised a small hand-held camera, and he snapped a picture of Devi before he turned slightly and took a picture of me. Perhaps he only records the life on the Nude Beach like I do, and I am one of the Odd Ones to him.

My thoughts returned to Eloise. Surely, I was one of the odd ones in the family to Eloise, even though we had become close friends after she contributed so much to my family research. She enjoyed discussing religion, and because she was so secure in her own immutable Christian faith, I could be honest with her about my agnosticism.

"I think you are a pantheist, Barbara, all that time you have spent on the river and in the mountains," chided Eloise. "It is a good thing to see God in nature, but nature is not the same as God." Eloise had been not been impressed at all by the link I had discovered between the Sutherland Scotch Grove immigrants of her ancestry and the Oregon Chinook through Archibald McDonald of the Hudson's Bay Company. "A lot of those Hudson Bay men married Indians," she said. "There were old stories about the Sinclairs who came to Iowa in the oxcart train with the Sutherlands—that one of them had a Cree Indian wife who was left behind in Canada when they came down the Red River Trail. I never heard of the Sutherlands having Indian wives although that might have been covered up. We considered even the rumors about the Sinclairs scandalous.

"Two of my father's uncles went to Oregon," she continued, "shortly after they came to Iowa with the family. They were all after adventure, you know, and they went to Oregon not to marry Indians but to fight in the Indian Wars." Then, correctly interpreting my silence as disapproval, she added, "Think of it this way, Barbara. If Archibald McDonald changed that Indian girl's name to Sunday, at least he probably made a Christian of her."

Eloise went back to talking about Robert. "Well, now, your father did a lot of bad things, there's no denying it, even though we all made excuses for him. But he always had big dreams, and they sounded so wonderful when he talked about them. It was a shame the way he left your mother alone with you kids and Bobbie with no daddy to look up to when he ran away to Colorado with Dorothy." The Minnesota cousin had left that morning and it was just the two of us, sitting in the darkened, hot apartment.

"You and your brother had to grow up in a shadow, all right, but you had your grandma's garden to go back to in that big old farmhouse. Your mom was a Hughes, real educated with that Hughes money and land behind her, not like that Dorothy Robert ran off with to Colorado." I didn't answer but the wheels in Eloise's mind continued to spin at a slower pace. "Dorothy left that first little girl she had with the Moats boy—probably didn't even look back. Now what kind of mother would do that? She was in and out of the mental institution at Independence, you know. Those girls that your dad had with Dorothy, technically your half-sisters, I suppose, didn't they end up in an orphanage?"

With that, Eloise had fallen silent and gave every appearance of being asleep.

That had been a relief, actually. I didn't want to argue about Indians, especially not Northwest natives that Eloise's great-uncles had come west to kill, and I'd already had the sermon about going to find my brother. It was getting late, and my plane would leave early in the morning. And I didn't want to talk about the half-sisters. I didn't want more siblings; I had enough to worry about just with my missing brother. I was feeling rather uncharitable toward my elderly cousin; in fact, I recorded Eloise's remark in my notebook:

"If Archibald McDonald changed that Indian girl's name to Sunday, at least he probably made a Christian of her."

Upon my return home, I scoured my sources for how the natives might have felt about Christianity. I found little record of their viewpoint, although Eloise's attitude had lots of company. In his journal of his 1834 travels down the Columbia, the naturalist John Townsend wrote disparagingly of native religion as mere superstition "in all its absurd and most revolting aspects . . . They believe in 'black spirits, and white, blue spirits, and grey,' and to each grizzly monster some peculiar virtue or ghastly terror is attributed." Townsend spoke hopefully of the potential for the Presbyterian missionaries at Walla Walla, the same missionaries who were famously massacred more than a decade later, to redeem the natives "from the thralldom of vice, superstition, and indolence."

I felt uncomfortable judging Eloise, who had been a spiritual mentor of my youth and had simply reflected the prejudices of her own time and faith in her remark. Was my use of the word "Indian" reflecting some insensitivity of my own? How did we know for sure that we had escaped the prejudices instilled in our childhood? As I gathered the dogs and returned to the car, I thought of the man in the Blue House who waited for the red in the sunrise that was not going to materialize that morning. Were we all the "Odd Ones" to each other?

"Our Country for Christ" was the motto on a Sunday school notebook that had surfaced in my earlier research of the Scotch Grove church. Surely it would have been possible to regard others as odd without violating their uniqueness, as the Christians had done with unbridled impunity. Notes from my winter reading illustrated that the natives of Wapato Island, who had been accommodating and friendly toward the Europeans, were not treated with respect.

The Cath-lah-min-na-min village on Wapato Island possessed a large sacred object: a block of black basalt that had been chiseled into a column about five feet in height and three in diameter. The natives believed that it had magical powers and to touch it would bring rain, so they treated it with respect. One of the Hudson's Bay Company men from a party that stopped at the village had tried to remove it, and a violent storm with considerable rain ensued, proving the natives right. After the village was dead from the Great Pestilence, the farmer who took over the land got tired of plowing around the sacred basalt pillar and finally rolled it over the bank.

And as for the young, beautiful Raven, Archibald McDonald's wife, who had died after giving birth to his child—had she by choice taken the name of Sunday? Raven was a powerful totem within her own culture and who knew what had been lost by the change? Consider the steadfastness of Chief Cassino.

In *Wappato Indians,* Roy Franklin Jones referred to Chief Cassino as an "outstanding native leader" in the old beliefs. "Chief Cassino listened and watched, but withheld judgment." This was after the Great Pestilence had decimated their numbers and he had taken up residence by Fort Vancouver. To his few remaining people he said: "Follow the priest if you like . . . I am unable to change" (*Wappato Indians,* 94).

❧

Our lunch that day at the John Street Café began with horses.

Madeline and I had just seen a film entitled *Buck* about a man who trained horses. He traveled around the country giving four-day clinics about natural horsemanship that neither of us could afford, even if we'd had horses of our own. When he was a child, Buck had been physically abused. His alcoholic father had whipped him and his brother until they had welts on their backs and finally they were removed from their home. As an adult, however, Buck was gentle and kind with people and horses and he adored his daughters and his wife.

"Buck must not have had a flattened orbital cortex," I observed as we waited for our order at the John Street Café. "And his amygdala must have been in good shape, too. With that kind of abuse he surely could have turned violent, like those serial killers in the radio study that started me down the futile genetic path to understand my brother."

"It's like Buck said, Barbara, he made the choice that he didn't want to be anything like his father."

I had to think about that.

"A genetic connection to problems would be easier in my family than in yours," continued Madeline. Her brother had been born with a particular shape to his mouth that resulted in a severe speech impediment and related health issues like chronic bronchitis.

"You knew for sure it was genetic?"

"Yes, we knew for sure," said Madeline matter-of-factly. Oregon Health and Science University had done a study for them.

"I've pretty much given up on any genetic explanation for my brother's behavior," I admitted. "If my father was dealing with a damaged brain it was probably from a traumatic birth instead of genetics." I had discussed this again with Eloise when she gave the inevitable you-are-your-brother's-keeper lecture.

"I know you'd like to think there was some strange genetic factor that accounts for your brother's failures, and it would be convenient to blame it on your father," Eloise had said. "In all honesty, Barbara, Bobbie might look like your father and he certainly acted like him, but you are the one with the genetic resemblance. Whenever I hear that you're climbing mountains, off again to some foreign country like Nepal where you have gone to my notion way too many times and I simply cannot fathom why you are talking about going there again, and now writing books, I think to myself—now that's her dad in her. He was so creative and full of such energy that he absolutely sought out adventure." Eloise's feet thumped the hassock as she focused in on exactly the comparison she wanted to make. "All those crazy stories that Uncle Arthur and Aunt Kitsy called lies! They weren't lies; they were imagination. Why, I was so pleased when you did that reading from your book at your grandma's old farmhouse and the whole community came. She's the best of Robert, I thought, as you stood there on the porch. Maybe if your dad had found mountains to climb or had his attentions turned to writing books instead of farming he would have stayed out of trouble."

"How did you lose track of your brother, Madeline?" I asked. Madeline told a sad story, a variation on my own family tragedy. In high school her brother had started running away from home, then getting into serious trouble. Always he was caught—in fact, it seemed that he wanted to be caught. As soon as the arresting officers heard him speak they decided this was a mental issue so instead of putting him in jail they shipped him to the Oregon State Mental Hospital. Always he walked away. This became a pattern for his life.

"Did you worry about him?"

"At first, I suppose, but I was young."

Yes, I knew how that went. I had been young, too, trying to get my own life in order when things went awry for my brother.

Had I worried about Bobbie? Sometimes. In fact, I forgot him for months at a time.

At one point Madeline's brother actually came back and lived with her mother for a while, got a job in a restaurant where he didn't need to talk to the diners. He seemed to have settled into a life of stability, but that's when her mother realized he was drinking a lot.

Ah yes, drinking a lot.

One day, out of the blue, Madeline's brother simply went missing. He had a DUI and was to appear in court. "That was some thirty years ago," said Madeline.

"Did you ever look for him at all?"

"My mother did before she died," said Madeline. That had been fifteen years ago, but the people in the government office they consulted weren't allowed to give out specifics. "I have imagined he might be dead—one of those nameless bodies of homeless men they find behind dumpsters."

For years I had imagined that, too, every time I saw a man with the lower half of his back exposed, sleeping under one of the I-84 bridges. This was becoming too uncomfortable for both of us. "What a strange coincidence that we both have missing brothers. I guess lots of families do, but mostly they don't talk about it," I remarked lamely.

So we tried to talk about writing.

"If I were writing fiction I could change things, but nonfiction is so inconvenient and inconclusive," I complained to Madeline in the gentle light from the big windows at the John Street Café. "Even with issues I thought I had settled in previous research." I proceeded to summarize a series of phone calls that had come in the last month from my distant and little-known half-sisters that had raised baffling questions for me. Was my father, our father, I meant, capable of violence, and how did he die? In all the research I had done, in all the family interviews, court records, and newspaper clippings, his death was never referred to as anything but a suicide. Now it turned out that it might have been murder instead. I sighed. To resolve this question in nonfiction I'd have to dig once more through all sorts of police reports, court records, when anyone who really knew the situation, if anyone really did, was no doubt already dead. In fiction I could make up a lively story using my father's liquor runs during Prohibition between Chicago and Minneapolis, his gambling debts, or even another disgruntled husband who found out my father was fooling around with his wife. "Well, you see what I mean, that in fiction you have the advantage after all and are not left with all these hanging threads that occur in real life."

"I am not exactly a divine entity who can entirely control events," countered Madeline, "you know it's more complicated than that." And I did, of course, but I was feeling sorry for myself.

"But at least you can make it come together. I'm left with a theme that life is a series of mysteries and many of them can never be fully resolved." Both of us were feeling a little irritable because we had not written in several days. Fiction or nonfiction, it was difficult subduing the unruly language that galloped around in our minds, requiring writing and rewriting, to get it to say exactly what we wanted it to say.

It was easier to talk about horses.

"My friend Anne with the Lipizzaner horses has invited me to watch her lesson on Patriot," said Madeline. "I could ask to bring you along," she offered.

"Oh, please do," I said. My mind flooded with a picture from a childhood book, a flying white stallion. "Does your friend train for shows?"

"I don't think so. I've never heard about any shows."

"Then why does she still take lessons?"

"The challenge, I suppose—for her and for the horse." Madeline explained a whole intellectual dimension of riding that had never occurred to me, a sophisticated communication between rider and horse built on a system of mutually understood signals.

I had only ridden horses on the farm—a flick of the reins, a nudge with the heel, and off we loped across the field. How difficult this sounded, a practiced skill with certain rules, more than a natural thing; something that took concentrated practice to do right, like writing a book. Not just riding a horse, but the art of riding a horse.

As we walked to the cars, our talk again turned to brothers.

"Were you close to your brother, Madeline, when you were children?" Bobbie and I had been inseparable as youngsters on the farm in the forties and fifties when there was not even television.

"Sort of." She had always defended him at school, she said, and she made her friends include him in games. People thought they were twins, both of them towheads and nearly the same size. She'd played the role of his protective older sister, interpreting his speech for others. When he was sick with bronchitis she brought the radio into his room. "He was in the bed, and I'd lie on the floor, and we'd listen to the Lone Ranger."

Yes, the Lone Ranger. I pictured the two of us lying together on the green rug of the living room floor, Bobbie with his chin cupped in his hand. The big table radio had a rounded top.

"We listened to that, too, and Gene Autry. I'm back in the saddle again."

Madeline got in her car but she opened the window and her voice lowered ominously. "And the Shadow . . . only the Shadow knows."

☙

Often the dogs and I left the houseboat well before five o'clock now, just as first sun was turning the thin fog over the river into blended colors. As we went up the ramp to the mainland, a great blue heron stood on the power line that led to the moorage, an oversized cardboard cutout against the brilliant purple and red of the eastern sky. Oregon was trying hard to redeem itself after the prolonged rain of June that had all of us restless. I would have liked to linger a few more minutes in the mist that was kaleidoscopically changing color, but the dogs were anxious to run. As I drove across the island to their excited warbling and barking, it was all so beautiful that I began to hum a line from a childhood hymn. "The morning light, dum-de-dum-dum-dum, what wonders God has wrought."

I had come back from yet another visit to Eloise (they were required every few weeks now as her health worsened) with a lot of that old music in my mind because she was given to bursting into spontaneous song. But by the time I had reached the Nude Beach, and the dogs tumbled out of the car, racing each other to the edge of the Columbia, which was as smooth as a sheet of mercury this morning and seemed to brim lightly over the sand and quiver in the rising mist, it was that last John Street conversation with Madeline I was thinking about. How had we gone so long without looking for our brothers?

One college summer when I was working at a camp in northern Wisconsin, I dreamed that my brother was dead, that he had been killed in an automobile accident. The next morning I left my job and drove all the way home to make sure he was all right. I had read Sophocles's *Antigone* that year at school: In order to bury her brother as required by ancient Greek religious ritual, Antigone had been willing to suffer the censure of the state and face certain execution. How romantic that sounded then, that Antigone had put duty to the family above any other consideration, especially above duty to the laws of the state.

But when I was in graduate school I read another *Antigone*, a translation from Jean Anouilh's French modernization of the conflict between youthful idealism and the limitations of politics. This version of the ancient drama confused me. Creon, the king of Thebes, seemed more rational in his arguments, more grounded in reality, than the hysterical, young Antigone. Exactly what purpose was served by Antigone's devotion to familial and religious duty? Or was it even duty? It seemed more an intense emotional stubbornness, a rash statement of rebellion. Would her capitulation to the laws of the state have been the end of youth or the beginning of adulthood? "Life flows like water," Creon had said to his niece when he advised her to not jeopardize her own brief happiness for a brother who had thrown away everything that was meaningful in his life.

Had Madeline and I ignored our brothers because we felt they had thrown away everything meaningful in their lives?

"It's like Buck said, Barbara, he made the choice that he didn't want to be anything like his father." That had been Madeline's line, but it was about violence, not addiction.

Was it always a choice, how we lived our lives? On an intellectual level I knew that chemical addiction was not a choice, but certainly I'd been inculcated by church and family that it was. Did I still believe that in my heart and was that why I didn't seek out my brother? Was it not by choice that he removed himself from our lives? He knows where I am, I had said almost angrily to my cousin Vaneta. He could get in touch with me if he wanted to.

Devi yapped wildly, spinning in circles as a Western gull, searching for garbage left by the sunbathers, wheeled lazily overhead. The white coats of the dogs turned golden in the morning light.

The last thing in the world my brother would have chosen was to be like his father: to leave his sons as he, himself, had been left.

I wrote his name in the sand. Then, as usual, I wrote the name Robert, and I thought of the surprising phone conversations with the half-sisters. Yes, I would think about my father; it was easier to think about a father who was already safely dead than a brother who was still alive and might need my assistance. Except this father was suddenly not so safely dead, and what was I to do about that? The half-sisters thought he was murdered. This is like Meriwether Lewis, I thought with something akin to annoyance. Here were the relatives, years later, wanting to dig him up. I was most assuredly not interested in disinterment. Did I need to get to the truth of this matter, and how would I do so?

Well, write about it, of course, I thought. At least that would clarify matters in my mind as to how much I needed to bother about this. Were these half-sisters family to me? I had taken extensive notes during the phone conversations with them. I would write this in the same way I had written the story about my father and the milking of the cow; I would write it from the notes I had taken at the time. Would it be fiction or nonfiction, and would that matter? "You can write the truth in fiction; sometimes it's even more effective that way." I better not tell Madeline how dependent I was becoming on her for direction or she would stop talking to me.

Before we finished the walk, three large container ships headed for the Port of Portland came upriver, taking advantage of the incoming tide. *Pacific Basin* was written on one's side in giant letters. Chasing the waves of the successive wakes had finally reduced Devi to exhaustion. The dogs flopped down beside me as I sat on a log and recorded the last of the morning's entry into the notebook.

Columns of fog rise from the river in spirals like dancing ghosts.

Life flows like water.

◌

What could I call this one? Not Men in the Family, but Conversations with Half-Sisters, I decided and put that at the top of the page. If I included myself (as myself) was it fiction or nonfiction? Conversations in memoirs were tricky—even Vivian Gornick, the academic "queen of memoirs," had ended up in trouble on that one when she admitted that her seminal conversation with her mother in *Fierce Attachments* was actually a composite of their exchanges. I'd heard a radio discussion about it. Was it fiction or nonfiction when an author did that, asked the interviewer of the critic who had summarily sniffed in derision. When an author uses a composite instead of an actual conversation, said the critic, we have a term for it: fiction. I glanced at several pages of scribbled notes I had made while talking with these women. Well, call it fiction, then; I couldn't remember every exact word of conversations that hadn't been taped. If it ever mattered I would work it out later; I was really just writing this down to clear out my mind.

Conversations with Half-Sisters

I could not think of Roberta as Bobby or even call her that, as Bobbie was the name I still used for my brother. When our father addressed the little dark-haired girl as Bobby, had he ever thought of the little dark-haired boy named Bobbie, whom he had left behind?

Having worked out my troubled family history to my satisfaction, once I had written about it, I wanted to move on. But according to Roberta, who had taken to calling me each Sunday and waxing expansively on the subject, for her and for her two sisters, my book had been more of a beginning. They had known so little about their biological father, Roberta said, that they read every bit of information about him with relish. They had thought of their mother's third husband as their father. Daddy Ralph, they called him, and they vied for his attention and love. But Daddy Bob as a presence was always there, Roberta insisted. Her mother had once told her that she continued to love him all her life.

Really, I said. I had been thinking of how to get out of this conversation without hurting Roberta's feelings because it was nearly time for the afternoon dog walk, but I was intrigued by this information. This undying love for Robert had been reported of my own mother as well.

Oh, yes. In every argument with Daddy Ralph, Mom would scream that Bob never would have treated her like that, that Bob was gentle and kind and good to her. So good, Daddy Ralph would holler back, that he put those little girls in an orphanage and took off west again to play at being a cowboy. And where's Bob now, he would taunt.

Do you have any memory of him at all, Roberta?

Not really, and neither does Betty Jean. Billie Jo remembers a couple of things. We were talking about it when we read your book and we only share one memory that we're sure involved him.

I waited. Roberta had skirted around this before in previous phone calls without telling the story.

Roberta wasn't absolutely sure what had happened, she said, but they all remembered the incident—well, she wasn't sure how Betty Jean could have honestly remembered it as Betty was just a baby then, and maybe she had heard the others talk about the incident later so many times that she thought she remembered it. Their memory went like this, only she was not totally sure, she said, whether Billie Mae had added details and now she had incorporated them as her own. In fact, she wasn't sure about much of anything because it was so long ago.

By now it felt like the story was not forthcoming this time either, and I was beginning to think of other things.

Roberta spoke hurriedly then, sensing my impatience with her stalling and fearing that the moment for dramatic impact had passed. There had been a loud knock at the door, and when her mother answered it, she immediately began screaming. The three children, huddled behind her, got a glimpse of a man's trousers from the knees down as their mother slammed the door shut. Their mother shoved them behind the couch and threw a blanket over them. Keep the baby quiet, keep the baby quiet, she hissed at them repeatedly. There was more pounding on the door, and Dorothy screeched, go away, go away, I have nothing more to say to you, it's all been said, there is no need for you to ever come here again, and she did not open the door. There must have been a bolt that kept the door shut as well as the chair Dorothy wedged against the knob, because the pounding was hard and loud. They stayed behind the couch, and Roberta remembered putting her hand over the baby's mouth so she wouldn't scream.

Why was Dorothy so frightened? I was sorry I had let my impatience show, and now I questioned with genuine interest.

It was Daddy Bob, and he had a gun.

A gun? Did you see the gun?

No, but Mom kept saying, stay down, stay down, he has a gun. She tried to pull a drape at the window, but it wouldn't close all the way.

So she saw a gun, then?

Don't you think she must have seen it or she wouldn't have said that? Roberta sensed my renewed interest, and her voice became more dramatic. But we all remember being very afraid we were going to be killed. Billie remembers the first part differently. I know I dreamed about a man at the door afterwards, so I could never tell you exactly how much of what I remember is true and what part of it is a dream. Daddy Bob came back, we told each other, and he was going to kill us. We talked about it for years.

So did . . . Bob . . . that is, Robert—why was his name so awkward even yet—did he go away?

We don't remember exactly except we are sure that he never broke into the house.

Did you ask your mother about this later?

The one time I tried to talk with her about it she had just come out of the hospital. I think they had given her some kind of electrical shock treatments. She didn't remember quite what happened, and she didn't want to talk about it. That was long ago, she said. Just forget about it.

Could you ask her now? I had never heard any story about my father—our father—that had implied he was likely to commit any kind of violence to others. I knew Dorothy was still alive, although in an institution again, but I had not sought her out for research. She was one woman among several, and contact would have seemed disloyal to my mother. Roberta had told me in another phone call that she had given Dorothy the book I had written, which included an account of my father's scandalous behavior when he and Dorothy stole my mother's car and drove to Colorado. Her mother read it eagerly, carried it triumphantly to her mental health group and showed it off. I'm in this book. I'm the woman she called Edith, Dorothy reportedly had said. It's all true. It's all true. Everything in this book is true.

Mom's pretty ill now. We don't really expect her to make it this time.

I should be appalled that I did not express any sympathy when Roberta said that, but the words did not come. The other players in that drama had been dead a long time, and Dorothy was a woman I had secretly wished dead all through my childhood. As long as Roberta was telling stories, I decided to ask questions.

If that is indeed your only memory of him, it is not a very happy memory. Do you remember being put in an orphanage?

No, Roberta said, we were so little then—I think Betty was just a baby—that I don't remember the orphanage at all; what I remember is going to Grandma Minnie's whenever Mom had a really bad spell. I remember the time Grandpa Ben took us to the Scotch Grove church and we saw you. We were all excited because you were our sister.

My memory of that encounter was of the damp smell of the church basement because the dehumidifier had quit working and a standing puddle of water was left under it. And I was aware of my mother's confused embarrassment at having her husband's children by another woman in her Sunday school class.

I guess Dorothy wasn't there?

I don't know, probably not. She was in and out of institutions several times that I remember. She always took medicine. Once when Mom was talking crazy we took her to the doctor, and we all sat in the waiting room. The doctor came out of his office and asked

Daddy Ralph to sign some papers. I heard him say that Mom should not go home right now, that she should stay in the hospital because he couldn't guarantee the safety of the rest of the family.

My god, had Dorothy threatened to kill you?

Something like that, I suppose. Mom must have said something that scared the doctor into having her committed right away. Billie was old enough to remember this quite well, and she says that the doctor told Daddy Ralph that he feared the family would be dead in a week. Sometimes our mom heard voices like Grandma Minnie.

Were you afraid of her?

Not really, Roberta said pensively. She could be awfully nice when she wasn't sick. It's a family thing, you know. Grandma Minnie was in institutions, too. My daughter has told me a couple of times when she was angry that she thinks I inherited the problem.

Did you?

No, I don't think so, even though I get really depressed sometimes. I don't exactly hear voices. At least I never had to go into an institution.

Sometime after the first barrage of phone calls from my dark-haired half-sister, my other half-sisters, Betty Mae and Billie Jean, had called, probably at Roberta's insistence. Betsy, the child Dorothy left behind when she and my father hightailed it to Colorado from Iowa in that car that my mother had bought with her teaching money, called too. My notes from those phone calls weren't as complete as the ones I'd taken when I talked with Roberta. It was not a time in my life when I wanted to expand complicated family ties, but I felt a strange tenderness toward Roberta, whose hunger for information and connection was apparent in the frequent phone calls. Roberta's life seemed somewhat like the life I would have lived had I stayed in Iowa and married a farmer: bearing three children, helping with the fieldwork, milking cows and feeding pigs. Roberta's children were grown now, her husband just diagnosed with Parkinson's disease. The loneliness of a farmer's life even in the Internet age was palpable, and the thought made me nervous.

Betty Jean, the youngest of the half-sisters, was grateful for the information about their biological father that they gleaned from my book. She, too, lived in the Midwest with her husband. She had no memory of her biological father Robert at all, no memory of the orphanage, and she considered Daddy Ralph her real father because he was there when they needed him. But she considered me a real sister, just as she considered Betsy, the little girl who had remained with her former in-laws when her mother ran away with Daddy Bob, a real sister, too. Did I know about Betsy, the little girl their mother had left behind?

Yes, I knew about Betsy. In fact I had heard tidbits about Betsy all my life, but of course I was not related to her and had never met her.

We'll have to get together some day, said Betty Jean. All of us sisters.

Billie Mae, who was the oldest of the three half-sisters, called from Florida. She was especially glad to read all about Daddy Bob in the book, she said, because she was very involved in tracing family roots. She and her husband had converted to Mormonism in 1964, she said, and she was serving the church now as a missionary through ancestry.com. She would be glad to forward all the family material. Yes, she actually remembered a little about Daddy Bob. She remembered once when he was walking down the street with her and her two sisters that she got a little in front of the others and he said, "Where do you think you're going, Daddy Longlegs?" Wasn't memory just the strangest thing? Why, she could even hear his exact voice in that memory. And of course, she remembered the time that he came to the door with a gun. I was the oldest, you know, so I remember more than the little ones, she said. Mom told me to run out the back door and get the neighbor, but when I looked out another man was there so I didn't go.

Were you sure it was him? Robert? I mean . . . Bob?
I know I asked that.

Oh yes, she was sure, even though he had a red handkerchief over his face. He was going to kill them, but instead he killed himself later that night, except her mother never believed that he killed himself. Her

mother thought that he was killed by someone he owed money to, because he had debts all over the county.

Really? That his death wasn't a suicide?

I'd never heard anything like that. All my young life I'd felt shame about the suicide, and later I had become quite obsessed with it.

Oh yes, lots of people thought that, Billie insisted. In fact, Daddy Ralph always said he paid off some of Daddy Bob's gambling debts so the rest of us would be safe. We girls met Daddy Bob's younger brothers, Harold, the one who died of a brain tumor when we were little, and the next one, Arthur Paul. Uncle Arthur, we call him now, because we talked with him again after we grew up, and he told us that no one in the family thought Daddy Bob really killed himself, at least not on purpose.

How odd, I thought, as she elaborated on this theory. I wonder why no one mentioned this apparent mystery to me when I was doing research on the family. The coroner's report listed suicide by carbon monoxide poisoning, but there had been no autopsy. I'd have to ask Eloise.

Billie Mae remembered the time their mother, Dorothy, a schizophrenic, was going to kill them, too. Oh, brother, that was a bad one, said Billie Mae. She was actually out of the house by then but she was scared for the rest of them and Daddy Ralph had talked with her about it. He was an awfully good man, Daddy Ralph was, she said, for all he did for them. Billie didn't remember the orphanage, either, even though it seemed like maybe she should remember something about it, as she was older than the rest of them. Little kids get blank spots in their memory, you know, when things are too sad to think about. Then she got a signal on her phone for an in-coming call from ancestry.com, which, she said, had become her mission in life now, so she needed to cut the conversation short. Just remember, Barbara, she said in parting, you're really my sister now.

A few days later I got a call from Betsy.

Betsy?

You don't know me, Barbara, but I know you now through your
book about the family. I'm the little girl Dorothy left behind when she
took off for Colorado with your dad.

Oh, yes—Betsy.
This time I took careful notes.

Bobby sent me a copy of your book. You know, I never knew
Bobby or Betty Jean or Billie Mae when we were children. My dad's
family wouldn't let me even go close to my real mom because they
thought the craziness would rub off on me. But just a few years ago,
after my dad died, I got in touch with them. It was so much fun, and
I met my real mother, too, you know, Dorothy. She cried and said she
had never wanted to leave me and worried about me a lot. Dorothy
died recently, you know. But the reason I called you is that I just wanted
you to know that I felt so close to you when I read that book because
of your love of horses. Horses are my life.

Really?

Oh, yes, I really do believe that God speaks to us through horses.

You do? I didn't want to indicate disrespect, but I certainly found
this attitude surprising.

Oh, yes, Barbara, He does, He really does and each horse is a
sacred vessel. Lots of other people think this way, too, and I'm in touch
with them through websites about horses. I ride every day with a wonderful man, and I think I am falling in love with him. This is inconvenient
considering my current matrimonial state, but I'm sure that God will
show us the way through this to happiness. God's plan is that we all
should find happiness. He will speak to me through my horse, and I will
know what action to take. He did that when I found Billie Mae, Bobby,
and Betty Jean and that brought us all happiness.

Ummm, I said. I wasn't sure what was expected of me here but
Betsy didn't seem to mind.

We're real sisters now, Billie and Bobby and Betty and Betsy. I feel like I can tell them anything about my life, and they will be on my side against the world. God wanted us to find each other so we could be real sisters. After reading your book and finding out how much you love horses, I feel like you are a real sister, too.

When I had exhausted the notes, I e-mailed the whole thing to Madeline. "Is this fiction or nonfiction? Are horses your life?"

Madeline ignored the first question, and it was almost a relief that she did not have all the answers, either. "Are horses my life? Good Lord, no," she e-mailed back. "Writing is my life. And God does *not* speak to me through horses."

Next I e-mailed the whole thing to my cousin Vaneta at Sweet Memories. "Do you know anything about this?" I asked. "Could this business with the gun be true?" Vaneta called me as soon as she finished reading what I had written.

"Good Lord, Barb. Let me think a minute," Vaneta said slowly. "I really can't imagine Uncle Bob with a gun or threating to harm anyone. I was just a child when he was married to your mom, but he always played with the kids at family get-togethers. He seemed gentle and kind, so much fun in a family where no one laughed much. He was so good with children." She paused.

Except his own, I thought.

"I feel rather sorry for Roberta. She's brave for reaching out to you. And I'm still thinking you should be careful what family you reject even when they don't seem much like family to you." She stopped again, and I knew what was coming.

"Most importantly, your brother. He's your real family, you know; I don't know about the half-sisters, you're on your own for that one. But not Bobbie. He is lock, stock, and barrel your full family; you spent your childhood together here in this very house—sleeping in the west bedroom waiting for Christmas morning, riding that horse together, going to the Scotch Grove Presbyterian Church."

I didn't trust myself to answer.

She continued slowly, as this was a sensitive subject between us. "Please go find your brother, Barb. Your mother would have wanted you to do that." Another long pause and then the most unkind cut of all.

"We all loved him once."

In July I didn't go to the Nude Beach in the afternoon at all because it was crowded, and my dogs were rude in unclothed company. Even early that morning there had been a man standing naked in a sun salutation yoga position. Pani ran right up behind him and stuck her nose in his not-so-private-on-the-nude-beach private parts. "Pani," I yelled, and the dog came back, but the man turned and faced me with friendly amusement.

"Sorry!" I called.

"Welcome any time," he replied, and he turned back to face the sun.

I should not have waited so late to come, I thought, although it was not yet seven o'clock, and I had been engrossed, still writing and thinking about my brother. Sunday, yes, I had forgotten it was a weekend, and sometimes when the weather was warm, large pleasure boats with inflatable rafts tied to them were anchored as close to the shore as the water depth permitted. The occupants came to the beach later in the day or in the cool summer evenings for parties. Slightly downstream from the Man-in-the-Salute-to-the-Sun position another nude sat cross-legged reading a book. The dogs ignored him and raced on down the beach after swallows that swooped in figure-eight patterns. I moved back from the immediate shore and called them to keep them from barking too near the boats.

The Man-with-the-Metal-Detector who was not nude was already at the place where the volleyball net was sometimes strung and the dogs gamboled up in greeting. I had not seen him since early spring, when I last came to the Nude Beach in the afternoon. "If they play volleyball in the nude, how can you find anything here?" I asked.

"It's where they drop their clothes that I look," he said, and even as we spoke his metal detector pinged, and he picked up a quarter." Pani crouched in the play position and barked at the strange sounding machine. "You ought to see them come out and fling their clothes around—they don't think of nothin' but gettin' back to basics as fast as they can. You know," he said, momentarily distracted from his task, "I really think that for some people clothes are just a mask, and they need to be naked to show what they really are. Maybe it's the only time they feel natural. I've seen everything out here and I mean everything. You don't come here at night, do you? It wouldn't be safe for you then, even with the dogs. I've seen some real bad stuff with people drinkin' and fightin' here at night."

"No, I don't come here at night," I said. "I've been warned against that before. In the summer I don't even come in the afternoon." I walked on with the dogs but I had a sudden image of my usual early morning Garden of Eden scene on the beach turned into *The Garden of Earthly Delights*, a painting I remembered by Hieronymus Bosch.

Once when I had come on a winter afternoon, the sheriff deputy named Larry was just emerging from the beach. I did not release the dogs because I knew it was illegal and did not want to put him in a compromising position. "You be careful, Barb," he'd said to me that day, not because of the dogs but because they were looking for a man who had once lived on the island and was accused of shooting a policeman. "We've found more than one running from the law on this beach—it seems to be one of the first places they head. Don't you come here at night." He looked at the dogs with their anxious noses pressed against the window. "You be careful," he said again as he drove away. "I'm leaving now," he said in reference to my dogs. "I'm after more dangerous criminals than you."

When I reached the End of the Nude Beach sign with the dogs still bounding ahead on that warm morning I encountered the Man-in-the-Salute-to-the-Sun position, I saw that just beyond sign, the Builder was already busy at work on a structure that was actually more of a wigwam affair than his usual lean-to. Perhaps he was shy of the rowdy summer traffic, I thought, and I waved as I went a little beyond the sign myself. "No wind today," I called. "If anything, too much sun." His bare shoulders already looked a little red. He held a pole suspended in midair and regarded me gravely, as if I were being reckless. "We have to be ready for the wind," he said. I waved again and whistled for the dogs.

When I returned up the beach the man in the sun salute was gone but the other man sitting cross-legged was still reading. "Good morning," I said. "Good book you have there?" I did not write the names or any phrases in the sand even if the tide was coming in when there were people around on the beach.

"The Bible," he said. "The good book."

"A very good book," I answered, and then I called the dogs. Devi did not want to leave the beach and charged upriver again, racing a gull that flew in a straight line, low over the water. I was glad I was a long way from the boats because I had to blow the whistle to get her to come. The Bible? Was he telling the truth? Why did it seem odd to see a naked man in his morning meditation reading the Bible? Wasn't there some sort of injunction in Genesis about nudity? Not exactly, I decided when I looked it up later: "the eyes of them both were opened; and they knew that they were naked: and they sewed fig leaves together."

I was somewhat acquainted with the Bible, the King James version, anyway, because of the Scotch Grove Presbyterian Church. The small white wooden building had a bell tower that once pointed hopefully at heaven with a long slender shaft, but it had been later abbreviated to a squatty block because of a tornado. For many years my brother and I, our cousin Denamae Hughes, and a second cousin from our father's side, Jeanette Wilcox, formed what our Sunday school teacher Ella Clark called "The Faithful Four" while other community children came and went. We were rewarded for our memorization of Bible verses by a chart on the wall on which colored stars marked our progress. That morning at the Nude Beach, when I got back into my car with the dogs, I wrote from memory:

And the Lord said unto Cain, Where is Abel thy brother? And he said, I know not: Am I my brother's keeper (Genesis 4:9)?

"Do you know," Creon had asked Antigone in an attempt to dissuade her from wasting her own life to try to save one who had thrown away everything meaningful, "what your brother was?"

◌

An alcoholic. I was back in the houseboat, staring out my upstairs study window. My brother was an alcoholic who never could shake the addiction in spite of successive attempts to quit drinking. He had thrown away all the principles our mother and the Scotch Grove Presbyterian Church had tried to instill. Finally his wife had filed for divorce and left to deal with her own problems. He had betrayed his children, Robert and William, two boys the same ages as my sons, leaving them fatherless with nothing but a bank account from the land sale to provide some money each month for child support. For most of their childhood and adolescence, his sons had lived with their maternal grandparents.

The very last time I had heard from my brother was in the early 1980s when he had called me for money. I lived in Portland, Oregon, then, having gone through a divorce of my own that had been precipitated in part by my first husband's involvement in drugs. I was not feeling the least bit tolerant of any kind of chemical dependency. Bobbie was still in Iowa.

How much do you need? His phone call had taken me completely by surprise.

Five hundred dollars should do it, Barb.

I don't have five hundred dollars, Bobbie. I barely make it each month on my teaching check as it is, and I can't keep asking Jim for extra money. He and I have only been married for a year. He's awfully good about helping me hold things together when, after all, these aren't his children; they were part of the package deal. I have virtually no savings. What do you want five hundred dollars for?

This is hard to say, Barb, but I want to try another program.

To quit drinking? What happened with the last one?

It didn't stick, but I'm ready to try again.

I'm sorry, Bobbie, I don't have it.

That's okay, Barb. I don't want you to worry about it—I'll come up with it somehow. I've sold my part of the land now, but I've put it all in a fund for my boys.

He changed the subject without missing a beat. He never said anything mean about anyone, even his ex-wife.

So how are your kids? he asked.

"That must have been about the same time he came to see me at the Scotch Grove place," Eloise had said once before when we were sitting in her hot living room talking about Bobbie. "He asked me for five hundred dollars, too. Some kind of private dry-out program, I think, because he'd exhausted any army benefits by then."

"You know Barbara, we loved your brother like a son, Edwin and I did." They were well past the stage when they had to face the fact that much as they both had wanted them, they were never going to have any children of their own. "I'm not sure why God didn't see fit to give us any—maybe we were just plain too old when we got married—or maybe there was something else in the divine plan that made it that way, but it was a bitter pill." They never even discussed adoption because both of them felt so strongly about biological family.

After my brother had come back from the army, after I was gone from the community when our mother was dead, Bobbie always came around to see Edwin and Eloise. He and Edwin would sit in the yard after they'd played a game of croquet and have a beer together, Eloise told me. "Isn't that strange—that he'd play a game of croquet—such an old-fashioned approach to entertainment, more like we used to play at the Minnesota cabin on Green Lake when we went up there to see all the relatives." Sometimes she had to shake her head, Eloise confessed, because she could have sworn she was looking at Robert. "He not only looked just like his dad, he had his mannerisms, too, which seems impossible when Robert was long dead. Perhaps the most troubling aspect that reminded me of your father was the way Bobbie always had some grandiose scheme in mind, some big-rock-candy-mountain idea to make money. Edwin would caution him, try to say now have you thought of this or that, but in your brother's mind the big dreams had already had come true."

Several times Bobbie went to Minnesota during those years to see the grandparents we had barely known as children. "He was trying to be a Clark, I guess, and he was already getting the early white hair. We were usually there when he went, especially on the Fourth of July. Maybe it was his father Robert he wanted, I don't know about all that psychology business, but he was definitely a man who wanted his *father's* family, Barbara," said Eloise with conviction.

Apparently they wanted him, too. Our grandmother Kitsy, according to Eloise, even called him Robert sometimes, and our grandfather seemed glad to forget the past, to let go of some of the anger. They were all glad to see Bobbie get married, and then he and Karen had those darling little boys. "That little Robert, why he looked just like the other Roberts, just like his dad, and his grandfather, too, with that high forehead, the dark hair, and the blue, blue eyes."

Bobbie had a job, then, in Cedar Rapids, some sort of import company. And of course, he had the rent from land, both the land we had owned together from our maternal grandfather's estate and our mother's farm with its big house, which he and Karen rented out. There should have been plenty of money. "We didn't know he wasn't paying the taxes until it was published in the paper. That's when I first realized something was really wrong," said Eloise, "and that it involved drinking. Why, he never acted drunk around us," she assured me.

After that first DUI, Bobbie didn't come around to see Edwin and Eloise any more. "He was ashamed, I suppose. I think that really broke him, especially since they kept him in jail and then it was published in the *Monticello Express*. He had wanted so much to be liked, to be a respected man in the community, certainly not to bring shame on his family." Then the drinking was more obvious and became a topic of community conversations. Maybe they should have known it was coming because of the way he could put away beer, Eloise mused.

"You know, Barbara, I do believe he never drank a thing but beer. He learned it in the army, I guess. I feel sad about that because your mother was so proud of him serving the country—that was always a big thing in our community, you know. Most of us had military service in our family clear back to the Civil War. And I think he did well there—he was in some branch of the intelligence, I remember that. But I do think that's where Bobbie learned to drink. I saw a lot of that when I was in the Marines in California; why, they practically gave the men beer for nothing, and some of them put a lot of it away. I had a beer or two myself; of course, I never wrote my folks about that."

It was strange that no one thought they should write and tell me what was going on, how my brother's life was falling apart with the drinking and the divorce, but maybe no one even had my address. I was living in Greece then and going through my own troubles.

"If that was in the early eighties, then it was right after he talked to you that he came to me," Eloise said. "I could easily have given Bobbie the money then and maybe that program would have saved him." She paused for a moment. The love she felt for me, daughter of her favorite cousin, the love she had also felt for Bobbie, and her own desire to settle up unresolved issues before her imminent death gave her impunity in offering both criticism and advice.

"You should be ashamed of yourself for not helping him, Barbara, and so should I. It is on both of our souls that we gave up on him so easily, that we did not stay involved in his life. We failed him as family, as blood relatives who have a special obligation to those who are flawed. That is why it is absolutely imperative that you find him before I die. I'd gladly give you the money for it now. That time it might have saved him and changed his life."

"I don't want your money, Eloise," I said nervously. "It isn't a matter of money that I haven't looked for him." I was surprised to see that her eyes were so full that she fumbled for her handkerchief. Eloise looked out the window at hummingbirds challenging each other for the feeder with violent swoops. She was not the crying type and even had difficulty saying I love you in reply.

Why is that, Eloise, I had asked once. I'm sorry that we waited so long in our lives to form this intellectual companionship that is so satisfying for us both, even if I have to fly from Portland to Mesa to see you. My mother died when I was only twenty-one, and you had no children, so we could have had this companionship all through the years. Why can't you say you love me back when I know you do?

We never said those things out loud in our family, not the Clarks nor the Sutherlands, Barbara, but yes, you know I do, of course, and I wish I could show it more but I can't. But I could have shown it to Bobbie by giving him money when it might have saved his life. I felt somewhat differently about money in those days, and Edwin did, too. Whoever thought that we'd end up with so much of it and no one we wanted to give it away to when we died?

"I can still see Bobbie standing there in a pair of pants that needed mending, humiliated to be asking me for money," said Eloise. "That wasn't the way he wanted to be, I knew that. He used to bring beer over for Edwin, sometimes even candy or flowers for me. He wanted always, like his father had wanted, to be the one who gave presents to others, not the one who was asking for help. I was humiliated, too; when one in the family fails it is a family failure. God knows, we all felt that way with Robert a generation earlier. And now Bobbie was failing, too, and I felt a wave of shame go through me. Here's Robert all over again, I thought, and I told him so. You sound like your father, I said, like Robert himself, and he looked like I had slapped his face."

Now Eloise continued with genuine pain, looking out the window in a confession of what she viewed now as her own failing.

"I told him no about the money because I knew he would likely just use it for drink. We were all brought up that way, not that people needed help, but that it was a failure of self-control, it was a weakness. I still feel that way."

I had been inculcated with that as well, but I should know better, shouldn't I, after all the training I'd had. I knew what alcohol did to adolescents. But my brother? Did I still feel the way Eloise did when we were talking about family? Did that explain, really, my own reticence to find my brother? That I *blamed* him, judged him by a different standard? My own eyes filled with tears as I listened to Eloise.

"I gave him twenty dollars for gas and he took it so he must have been totally out of money. How's the corn crop coming, he asked, just like none of this ever happened, but I just turned and walked into the house. That's when he drove away and we never saw him again, none of us in the Scotch Grove community nor any of the relatives that I know of."

On the Nude Beach I'd picked up the bottles and spent needles that had been left from some after-dark party and left the plastic bag beside the portable toilet in the parking lot. Would these nighttime revelers join the long line of addictive behavior that would rob them of meaningful lives? It was not just of my brother I was thinking. I sat by my houseboat window that morning and flipped back through my notebook to find something I had paraphrased from the winter's reading.

At the time of Franchere's journey to Fort George on the Columbia, he observed that the natives regarded liquor as poison. One day a son of Chief Concomly came to Franchere's camp and one of the Europeans thought it amusing to convince the young man to imbibe a large quantity of wine. The drunken stupor produced lasted for two days, and Chief Concomly was not amused. He came to Franchere's camp and told them they had behaved dishonorably by making the young man drunk and exposing him to ridicule. The chief admonished the Europeans for this disgraceful practice and implored them not to supply any more liquor to the natives.

❧

By early August I could count on seeing at least one tent back in the cottonwoods on the Nude Beach and a boat or two anchored offshore. Camping anywhere on the island was illegal, but I wasn't going to turn anyone in, certainly not when I was running unleashed dogs. It was not unusual to see a sleeping bag that had every appearance of being occupied nestled against the log sides of the Blue House. If this was the Man-With-the-Camera, he did not show his face or his camera again, and the dogs stayed away from the makeshift shelter. The people who shared the beach with me in the pre-dawn beach hours probably shared my feeling of immunity from the perfunctory regulations that were clearly posted at each entrance. No camping. No dogs off the leash.

"Clothing optional" is what did it, I decided, even when you chose to wear your clothes, as I did. I stretched my arms above my head as the dogs raced off ahead of me. Such a relief, to be back on the Nude Beach on a beautiful morning, to feel at least the illusion of freedom, a step outside the normal confines of society. I waved at a woman who had emerged from her tent to watch the sunrise. How nice, I thought, that I was not the only one witnessing the silent golden flame sliding across the water. The blue fog between the Washington hills across the river began to fade. I found myself humming the song my father's brother Howard had sung in his wavering voice on the phone, that ridiculous song about a goat that had angered the farmer, who tied it to the railroad track. It had been running through my head since my last visit to Eloise. Just last week I had written the words I remembered in my notebook.

> The whistle blew;
> The train grew nigh.
> Bill Grogan's goat
> Was bound to die.

Eloise had been unequivocal regarding the new information from my half-sisters about her favorite cousin's death. "I wouldn't believe a thing those girls say, Barbara, not a thing," said Eloise. "They were just babies—even you were only in third grade when Robert died, so the oldest daughter of his second family was younger than that." The large thermometer that hung on the patio to accommodate Eloise's failing eyesight read 112 degrees, and inside the retirement apartment the air was stifling. "To be honest, I heard that story about someone threatening Dorothy with a gun, too."

So why didn't you tell me when I was working on the family book and had some of the research more readily at hand, I wanted to say. She seemed to have a selective memory at best. Eloise made no apology for the omission. "If someone came to Dorothy's door with a gun, it was those gangsters, trying to collect on gambling debts. We all knew Robert was a compulsive gambler, even if to this day I don't think any of the relatives—except me, of course—ever said it aloud, and I'm only saying it to you. Robert would never have threatened to kill anyone. He was the most gentle man, and he was if anything too courteous with women, always trying to bring gifts and please them."

Now Eloise wasn't saying that any of this misinformation was the fault of those girls, she insisted, and that they weren't perfectly good Christian women now, but remember that they had an unfortunate beginning, to say nothing of the fact that they got some craziness from both sides. Aunt Kitsy never let Robert bring Dorothy and her daughters into the house; Eloise knew that for a fact. "They had to stay at Harold's place when Robert went to see his mother, Harold told me so himself." In fact, Harold was the one who told her the gun story, and he certainly didn't believe Robert had anything to do with that—except the debts, of course, that these men might have been trying to collect from Dorothy.

Eloise stroked her chin thoughtfully. She interrupted her story to say, "I feel a whisker, Barbara, so I want you to take the tweezers and pull it out." I did, and Eloise continued.

"We all knew how kind Robert was; that was why we all forgave him so many transgressions. That's why women loved him so much. But naming one of the girls Roberta; how could he use the Robert name again? That Robert name is bad luck, no doubt about it, and I don't know what it will take to break the spell. You aren't in touch with your brother's children, are you? That first little boy was named Robert, too."

"No," I confessed glumly. I had been preoccupied with my own failing marriage when they were little, and then so ashamed of how my brother had left his family, that I never resumed contact with them at all.

"That doesn't speak well of you, Barbara. You are such a contradiction in terms; always so worried about world causes but totally ignoring your nephews." Eloise had perfected the skill of heaping on guilt.

"Now as for your father's suicide, Barbara, I know what a fascination that has had for you all your life. Such an unfortunate thing for a child, when a parent commits suicide. You wrote about it, you thought about it, and you even tried it yourself. That unhealthy flirtation with death is probably why you are still trying to climb those mountains that don't in the least need climbing by you."

Now that was an interesting thought. I remembered a passage from earlier writings that I had copied into my notebook after talking with the half-sisters.

In Oregon when I felt the dark seductive swirl pull down again I said to the psychiatrist, "I don't get it. Why am I still thinking about it? I thought that was all behind me." "Don't do it," she advised. "Your children will never get over it." And I never let myself think of suicide again, because the last thing in the world I wanted was for my kids to duck their heads in shame and confusion (*Prairie Reunion,* 120).

"No family wants to believe in a suicide," Eloise mused, "because it implies guilt for those left behind, that they might have helped avert the tragedy somehow. I know Harold didn't want to believe that his brother had taken his own life; he said so to me. Why, Robert relished the excitement of getting out of a scrape, he told me once; that was why he was always in one. Robert lived in a fantasy world where in the end, everything turned out right. He never would have killed himself." Suicide was such a disgrace in those days that Eloise was sure that my grandmother,

her poor Aunt Kitsy, never got over it. "Uncle Arthur wouldn't even let her come to the funeral, you know. It was his brothers who came to Iowa and held the service."

I remembered that, although I had been just a child. Our uncles Harold and Howard had stopped to see our mother at our grandmother's farmhouse where we lived. Bobbie had run up to car.

"Are you my daddy?" he had asked. Doesn't he know? I thought. Doesn't he know our daddy's dead (*Prairie Reunion,* 85)?

Eloise sat back in the chair for a moment, stroking her chin again. Then she leaned forward, speaking with intensity, abandoning the passive manner she often used in conveying information for which she did not want to claim full responsibility.

"But there was a coroner's report, Barbara. There was a hose attached to the car exhaust and put through the window. Maybe he knew the gangsters were going to kill him. And don't forget, there was a marriage license on the seat that hooked him up with a new woman in Colorado, and he could have been arrested for bigamy, never having formally divorced Dorothy. Either way, he was in a colossal mess, facing trouble every way he turned. The best I can do for him is to think that maybe he didn't really intend to die, that he thought that God, at the last moment, would reach down and pluck him from the car and once again get him out of his self-created mess like He reached down to Green Lake in Minnesota during the tornado when we were just kids and had gone out too far on the water." With that, Eloise sat back in her chair and pretended to go to sleep.

Now if I were writing fiction, I mused as I walked along the beach that morning, a murder by gambling thugs with a suicide merely rigged evidence to cover the crime would no doubt be a more colorful story than a real suicide. Maybe I should try my hand at fiction, after all. As I turned at the End of the Nude

Beach sign, the sun hit my face with full force, and my mood changed. Lives that had been actually lived were not fiction and should not be rewritten as such, I thought with sudden resentment. I did not want to be bound by the literary rules of fiction that required at least somewhat logical connections, a recognizable order of beginning, middle, and, finally, an end. Lives actually lived were full of inconsistencies and unsolved mysteries. In many situations a thoroughly honest resolution was impossible or at least hard to come by.

The sad part was not that my father died at thirty-seven, but that he had not lived up to his responsibilities and that he had wasted his life. Both my brother and I had been deeply influenced in unfortunate ways by this man we had never known. The *idea* of our father's suicide had nearly resulted in my own death at an early age when I harbored the romantic notion that death was the answer to anything. Mine was a lucky escape, and I had resolved any residual influence when I wrote about it. And I didn't agree with Eloise; I hadn't climbed mountains because I wanted to die. I had climbed mountains because I was determined to *live*.

But what about my brother? Whatever the issue had been for him, it had not been resolved in time. What idea had he harbored in his mind, as I had done with suicide, that had directed his life in such negative ways? Why had my brother gone time after time to Minnesota, seeking contact with our father's family? I had never done that; in fact, I lost touch with them for decades and felt the connection somewhat shameful; it mostly reminded me of my mother's lonely life.

I had come home from college in the early sixties making light of what a literature professor had called the "search for the father" theme in modern literature, but my mother was already worried about Bobbie, who had dropped out of school. My mother and I sat at the dining room table where I had just turned off the green-shaded lamp. More than forty years after her death,

I could still hear her voice in the darkened room. I sat down on a
log that had washed up on the beach. I opened my notebook and
wrote down what I remembered of her words.

A boy needs a father, my mother had said sadly. I couldn't make
up for that. When it became painfully apparent that we would be living
at Grandma's, I went to the house on the farm—my farm still, as my
father had given it to me at my marriage, although I had just rented it
on shares to Merle Huseman. I had things stored upstairs, and I must
have been looking for something. Your brother—he was such a bright
little boy—ran to the barn. Merle didn't keep milk cows at all so the
barn was dark, but the door was open. "Is my daddy here?" Bobbie
asked. By the second time we visited, he had changed the reality in
his mind. "My daddy is here milking the cows," he told me with firm
conviction even though he couldn't see into the barn, and if he had
been able to, there would have been no daddy and no cows. That is
when I felt a stab of fear that he would have trouble facing the truth like
his father. "No, Bobbie, your daddy is gone," I said emphatically. "The
cows are gone, too." Our finances were in such a mess, Barbara, I
thought I would never get things straightened out, but I finally did.

But my brother had never managed to get things straightened out. Like his absent father, he had lived in a fantasy, always
embellishing stories, telling things as he wanted them to be, not
as they really were, believing in the end that everything would
turn out all right. And he was always bringing presents, even
when he couldn't afford them. I had heard a story of him once
giving away one hundred dollar bills at a tavern, giving them
away to women with sad stories. Like our father, Bobbie had not
lived up to his responsibilities, and he had wasted his life. What
had gone through the minds of his children, two little boys, when
he faded out of their lives with their family finances in disarray?

"It is only our mother," I said as we lay there in the darkness. "She
buys the things in town." My brother was older than I, but he refused

to give up believing that Santa Claus came. He did not answer. A car came from the west and threw shadows of crooked limbs across the wall. I said it again. "No," he said, finally. "There is a man who comes. A big man who carries all the presents" (*Prairie Reunion,* 25).

Even Devi got tired of chasing gulls and came over to lie down with Pani. I reread what I remembered of my mother's words. Yes, the darkened barn, the search for the absent father through family connections, far more painful in real life than in any fictionalized account. In all honesty, I no longer cared how my father died; we were all bound to die. Let them dig up poor old Meriwether Lewis to see if he committed suicide or was murdered, I thought, glaring at the river where the famous explorer had once come past our island in his canoe. Lewis, too, had unresolved debts, psychological problems, and he drank too much. Why did it make any difference how he died? The important thing was that he had done extraordinary things with his life. I got up from the log, and the dogs followed me back to the car.

On the way back to the houseboat, however, I thought once more of Eloise and how that particular session had ended. When she awoke, after the tirade about my father's death, she had resumed her relentless campaign that it was my sisterly duty to go and find Bobbie.

"He is still your brother, Barbara."

Am I my brother's keeper?

I could never say that to Eloise. I was not going to get out of this, and I knew it. We all had grown up in the Scotch Grove Presbyterian Church.

Chapter Two

Too much death for only seventeen houseboats in the decade we'd been at the moorage, I told myself. After Smitty died, after his family had scattered his ashes in the river, and a double rainbow had obligingly come over the Channel at just the right time, I sat out on our deck for a while and then took a walk alone to think. About both death and the double rainbow, that is, and maybe I needed to think about souls and whether Smitty was headed downriver now in a fog canoe.

In James Agee's *Death in the Family*, the butterfly that coincidentally lifted from the coffin as if it were the man's soul seemed a flaw in an otherwise perfect piece of literature, in my opinion. Too convenient, I thought, although it likely happened that way, as that was an autobiographical novel. And now this double rainbow for Smitty. That was the trouble in nonfiction. Sometimes the coincidental truth seemed like fiction, like the fact that both Madeline and I had brothers missing for thirty years, and the coincidence had to be altered slightly or at least toned down or one would be accused of making it up. Perhaps the truth was possible *only* in fiction. I'd have to talk to Madeline about that.

If ever a soul was in tune with the river, Smitty's was, so if one had been inclined to believe in such things, it made perfect sense that at the moment when his ashes were scattered, some sign would be given. A skeptic could argue, of course, that it was still the season of rainbows, and they weren't that uncommon over the island, even double or triple rainbows. Lots of people had similar stories involving natural events that seemed significant when someone died. Madeline mentioned that seven geese flew in a line at a friend's funeral, a friend who had held the number seven in special significance. And one could certainly wish for some sign to observe Smitty's passing. Up and down the Mult-nomah Channel people loved Smitty, both for his building and fishing skills and for his generous heart.

The sudden surfacing of a sea lion would have been even more fitting for that gnarly old guy's watery leave-taking, I thought, but the sea lions only came early in the year, following the smelt and the spring chinook. No one at the moorage or the members of Smitty's family who had come from Idaho said anything about souls or religion like the uncle in Agee's novel, just that the tim-ing of the rainbow was perfect and that Smitty had deserved a colorful send-off. Still, a rainbow was a Biblical sign of some sort of future promise, and Eloise would no doubt see Smitty's rain-bows as such. I thought of a Nude Beach entry with multiple rainbows that I could use in a future discussion with her. Maybe she would see some sign, some promise of the future in that, too.

In the afternoon when the cold rain had kept everyone away from the beach, I saw a triple rainbow downriver, across from the mill smokestack at St. Helens. The sky broke just below the Blue House, the lean-to with the tarp stretched over the roof poles where I've seen the Man-with-the-Camera looking for the red sunrise three times and where I saw the Builder one day last week. He waved in greeting and smiled shyly. The dogs ran up to him, and he knelt to touch Pani, as if grateful for her nonjudgmental friendliness. I wanted him there today to see the show, this triple rainbow: the first large, colorful arch stood with ends on both sides of the river; the second rainbow plunged into the water just yards from each shore, and the third inside it was a mere wash of blended colors. What a waste that I was the only one to see this spectacular sight. Where are you? I called for the Builder, and the dogs ran back in surprise, thinking I meant for them to come . . .

When I first came to the moorage, I was charmed by the explosion of new life in the spring: the ducks that hatched in flower boxes, the baby beavers that sounded like human children complaining because breakfast was late as they played under the neighbor's tender shack, the fawns that pranced behind their mothers on the other side of the Channel, or even the coyote pups that tumbled from their den in the blackberries near the path that went around the string of wetland lakes in Wapato Park just down the road.

Soon that idyllic view had to be modified. Our son, who had come to see the houseboat, recognized the nature of the community right away. "Lovely view, Mom," he had said, "and great way of life with your kayak tied to the deck, but do you realize that you and Jim have moved to a retirement community? It's unique, to be sure, but the average age here must be pushing sixty-five." I had not thought of it like that at all, and he was exaggerating the age factor, I protested. Didn't he agree that most people here looked much younger than their age? Didn't they all chop their own wood and bring it down in carts from the parking lot? Why, even the eighty-year-old gal in number thirteen walked three miles around the nearby lake every day.

But it didn't take long to see that at this stage of the game things did change fast and without warning. First to go was Mike Denny, less than two years after we came. He was, in fact, not much older at all than I am now, and he had practically promised us not to die when we moved in. He was one of the owners of the moorage and had said, well, you can always ask me for help. You're safe till I go, and I'm not planning on goin' soon, he told us, when we expressed some apprehension about this new way of life. We knew nothing at all about keeping the chains that moored our house to the boardwalk in good shape so we wouldn't float down the river in a flood. Mike was the one who told the stories about Candy diving off the roof nude and Lorraine passing out on the ramp that led up to the parking lot. "I'll never know why Lorraine didn't fall off the boardwalk and drown 'cause she got drunk as a skunk every Thursday when she went up to North Portland to get that wig all curled up again—Miss Piggy, I call her," he said. "She always went drinkin' at the Portland Rose after her hair appointment."

Mike was working inside his metal shop on the lathe when he had some sort of stroke, and just like that he was dead before the next morning. How odd this is, said his wife Patty, who was in serious shock. This man who has been my very soul mate, the love of my life, dies, and I wake up the next morning thinking that now I will have both dressers for my clothes. I guess this is what they mean that today is the first day of the rest of your life.

The next to go was a man named John at the lower end of the boardwalk, a man we hadn't known well because he had just returned from Guam with his wife, who was beautiful but did not speak a single word of English. He had cancer of some sort, and my son reminded me later that, after all, we were just downstream from a superfund site in Linnton, which was a disquieting thought, so I decided not to think about it. Besides, John had spent most of his time in Guam so maybe he got cancer there. He and his wife moved away before he died, and they rented their houseboat to a Presbyterian minister.

Then Doug. He was younger than I was, so his unexpected death was the one that shook me up the most. He and Jo lived in the house at the downstream end of the boardwalk, only yards from the boat put-in where the car with the woman and baby had been brought to the surface when the new ramp was put in. Doug was a big strong man, a teddy-bear sort, soft spoken, a teacher who worked to remove land mines in Afghanistan so playing children would not lose their legs or even their lives. But just like that, even faster than Mike Denny, he was gone; he got up one morning and fell down by the bed with a massive aneurism, and when Jo woke up later he was already dead.

Dorothy, who had been eighty when we came and still walked three miles around the lake, got carted off by her well-meaning kids when they detected signs of Alzheimer's. Don't wait too long, Dorothy had told me just before she reluctantly left, or other people will take over your life. Jump off your deck into the river instead if you see them coming for you. So the next one I could actually count in moorage deaths since we had come was Lorraine.

Lorraine, who popped on a curly wig the minute she got out of bed, or maybe slept in it. She did look like Miss Piggy, Jim insisted, and that was even before Mike Denny told us he called her that. That second or so Thanksgiving in our early years at the moorage, we'd had an open house and everyone came. Lorraine, with that fake faded flower in her hair, planted herself at the dining room table with the food and greeted anyone who came in like she was the hostess herself. She offered everyone a drink even though she had given up the vice herself two years ago, she said; she had to because they'd found out she had only one kidney, and it was not working right and would soon kill her off. After three years in dialysis, it did. The Presbyterian minister, who had just rented John's house, introduced himself to Lorraine at the party. "You must be quite the gal," he said, smiling. "I hear you have been a long time on your houseboat and outlived three husbands." "I screwed them to death," Lorraine replied in her gravelly voice without batting an eye. It was her standard line to anyone new. "And every one of 'em died with a smile on his face."

After that it was Smitty and Arlene. They both had cancer for years, according to Patty Denny, but Arlene's was the most advanced, the worst form of lymphoma. Her hair came and went, but the disease was in a short-lived remission when we first moved in. "I've read your books," she said quietly. "The book I liked best was the Still Creek one about Jim and the two of you climbing all those mountains together. We've climbed our mountains together too, Smitty and I, not ones just like yours but mountains just the same. Jim sounds like Smitty, always doing the best, even by kids that weren't his own." Then Smitty died, too, and the whole river, not just the moorage, mourned. "One could do worse," Jim said, "than to live out your life by the river and then to die in your own houseboat with a beer in your hand."

It was a hot afternoon, and Jim was asleep on the couch, so I went for my walk alone, without even the dogs for company. I wanted to go where I had a possibility of seeing sandhill cranes, although it was really too soon for the big gray birds to return to the island. A. E. Housman had his cherry boughs, hung with snow each spring, and W. B. Yeats had his wild swans at Coole "wheeling in great broken rings" to remind him of the brevity of life, but sandhill cranes had become my measure of mortality with their seasonal migration.

So I drove to the fishing ramp at the big bend in the Gilbert River. This was close to where I'd heard the ghosts of the native women, or whatever the noises were, but this time I walked the other way from the parking lot, along a fishing path that followed the muddy river right to where it flows from Sturgeon Lake. In a few more weeks the whole area would be closed to all but hunters. I was surprised as I neared the end of the path to see a small, flat-bottomed rowboat anchored with no occupant in sight. It had no identification, so perhaps it was a Fish and Wildlife craft, I decided. I forgot about the boat as I reached the point of land where the river flows from the lake. Screened by the Oregon ash, I did not in the least disturb the plethora of birds in and across the water. The seasonal migration was coming early this year.

White pelicans preened their feathers as they perched on the half-submerged logs in the lake. A small flock of yellowlegs poked and bobbed on their golden stilts along a slanted sandbar not far from where I stood. On the lake skein after skein of newly arrived geese lifted and settled, lifted and settled in noisy clatter. I could hear no cranes, so I was probably too early for them, after all. In truth, I did not think of Smitty or the double rainbow or even about souls at all. I just sat down on the path and watched the busy waterfowl spectacle until the green-gold leaves of the

Oregon ash were back-lit with late afternoon sun before starting back toward my car.

As I passed the flat-bottomed boat again I was surprised to see that it was no longer deserted. Beside it, thigh deep in the water, stood a young woman—not that young, thirty-five or so, right at that age when a woman's body is at its best. She wore only a baseball cap, her hair tucked up under it, some strands curling down her neck in damp tendrils, her skin glowing golden like the ash leaves. How youthful this woman looked, I thought with no little envy. Why was she here instead of at the Nude Beach? Was some partner waiting for her to come and make love in the tall grass across the river? I smiled and waved my hand, and the young woman smiled and waved in return before she languidly turned back to the water as if feeling with her toes for something she had dropped.

As I reached the car I looked back, but the boat and woman could no longer be seen. My throat swelled with what seemed a missed opportunity. What would I have said, anyway? No doubt some inconsequential remark. Don't stand too long in the river or you might dissolve. Then you would float downstream—from the Gilbert River to the Multnomah Channel of the Willamette, to the Columbia, to the Pacific. Like the natives who lived on the island before us for thousands of years, and now Smitty. I thought of the fog canoes. Even the nude woman beside the boat whose youthful glow I had envied would soon die.

As I was standing there, four early sandhill cranes flew by in chortling conversation. I was so delighted that I clapped my hands. How appropriate, I thought, like Agee's butterfly or Smitty's rainbow, that cranes should fly low over my head, just when I was contemplating my advanced age against a young nude woman whom I imagined waiting for a lover. Was this some sort of sign to remind me of my own mortality, something to signify reoccurring cycles, or just some lucky coincidence?

Whatever it might have been, it made me glad. I felt my life fly past me—an old reel with a broken spring unraveling film, whirling the whole roll in an untidy coil around my feet. Joy and gratitude, that's what I felt, and I twirled around sharply, making myself so dizzy I had to sit down. Yes, joy, there was no other word for it. Joy for my perfectly unexemplary life, joy for each time I made love in unexpected places—sand, wild strawberry leaves, the north Cascades, even on snow.

"It goes too fast," I said aloud. "Life goes too fast."

◌

The call from the nursing home about my brother came shortly after Eloise decided to die. It had been a hectic end of the summer and early autumn, back and forth from Oregon to Mesa as Eloise demanded my presence and sent money for me to come. Why did I respond to each command of this distant cousin, I asked myself on one of the return plane rides. Surely I was not secretly hoping that Eloise would break her promise not to leave me any of the money? If so, I did not approve of myself. But whether or not that was any part of it, the real reason was the shared heritage, both the tie with my father that I had mined incessantly while writing my childhood memoir and the heritage of the Scotch Grove Presbyterian Church as well.

That spring Eloise had been diagnosed with acute myeloid lymphoma and started ultra-violet treatments. They were terribly expensive, lasted only a few seconds, and made her look as dark as the illegal aliens about whom all the old gals in her Arizona retirement community tirelessly complained, Eloise said, as if the place where they lived could even operate without them. Better her body falling apart than her mind; she had no patience at all with the vacant-eyed elderly who endlessly repeated the same questions. "I need you, Barbara, and you said you would come anytime I needed you, and I'm sending the money for the plane tickets whether you want it or not."

So I came, even when I did not approve of the purpose, such as the driver's license renewal. "I want you to take me to Motor Vehicles now," Eloise insisted. "If we wait until my ninety-fourth birthday, the macular degeneration will be even worse, and I won't be able to pass the eye exam."

"There's a bus that operates from your apartment complex. If you can't see you shouldn't drive."

"That is not an option."

One did not argue for long with Eloise. We had gone to the motor vehicles department in Mesa, and after an embarrassing episode when Eloise's walker got caught in the revolving door, and a scathing glance from the clerk that silently asked me why I was complicit in this impossible task, the license was denied because Eloise could not read the letters in the center of the chart. Then and there the clerk punched a hole in her license and issued her a government ID card. "I'm so sorry," he said before turning to help the next customer. He was used to this in Mesa, a location with more than its share of senior citizens. "Do you have a way home?"

We went through the revolving door to the car, and this time I helped Eloise into the passenger seat. Eloise hated it when I drove; she thought I was way too cautious. She was a fast and aggressive driver and only last month had managed to get a ticket for speeding reduced if she promised to go to safe driving classes. Usually, on the infrequent occasions when she allowed me to drive, she gave incessant directions, but now she didn't speak at all, merely motioned where I should turn, which was away from the street leading to her residence. At Apache Junction Eloise waved her left hand slightly, indicating that I should turn north. We went silent miles through saguaro cactus, at last turning east toward Globe. Finally, I could stand it no longer. "Losing one's license to drive is not the end of the world, Eloise," I said quietly.

"It's the end of my world, Barbara. I had previously decided on this as a sign; I had, in fact, prayed about it, so it is not as if I am circumventing God's intentions for me. Instead, I am fulfilling them."

"What do you mean by that?" I knew because we had discussed this before, but I wanted to hear Eloise say it to be sure her mind was clear.

At first Eloise didn't answer. She paused to look out the window at the desert landscape. "I wish it were still spring, Barbara. Remember how that hillside was covered with the bright golden poppies when we drove out here this spring?"

"I remember that," I said.

"We can wish for spring, but when it is past it is past. For every living thing, Barbara, there is a season, and my season of spring, of summer, and even of autumn is past. Winter is undeniably upon me. I want to die before my brain is destroyed, not after I have lost my capacity to think. God has left me with a clear mind for this very task."

I felt uncomfortable with Eloise's train of thought. I felt as if I was being asked to assist in a suicide, and I said so.

"Letting yourself die naturally by rejecting all the medicines that keep you alive artificially is not the same as taking your own life. Death is a natural part of life, and when we finally accept that, there is an element of relief. I have accepted it, and you should, too. I dream of a river again and again, Barbara, and on the other side are all those in the family who have already died. In my dream I reach out to them—my parents, my cousins, my husband—and I call to them, one by one. Robert, I call in my dream—"

"Robert? I presume this is heaven that you are imagining on the other bank of the river, and I find it hard to believe that you see my father there."

"You need to go back to church, Barbara, and I do not say that lightly. I have been respectful of your changing faith, but my time for religious advice has almost passed. Now I will admit that your father surely holds the record as the family sinner, but of course he is in heaven because he believed. Heaven is not about

keeping people out; it's about letting people in, bringing everyone together." Eloise's voice was more natural now.

"And the river, remember that old gospel hymn about gathering at the river—now we gather at the river? I don't remember
that we ever sang it much in church as it was far too emotional
for the Presbyterians." Eloise broke into a full-throated alto, and
for the first stanza at least, her voice was strong and young.

"The river is a primal image, Eloise. The shades on the other
side are the already dead like in the *Odyssey*. Or *Gilgamesh* and
the boatman Urshanabi with his long pole. Sometimes the river
carries the dead to the ocean. Our island natives positioned their
burial canoes to be carried by the Columbia River to the Pacific.
Sometimes, when I walk along the Nude Beach, I think of the
Columbia as the Jordan and, just for the fun of it, I carefully
peruse the fog on the Washington side." We were silent for a few
minutes, each thinking our own thoughts. "Eloise," I cried, overcome suddenly with a rush of emotion. "I love you, and I don't
want you to die."

"Oh, for heaven's sake, Barbara, stop it. I'm almost ninety-
four years old." But Eloise did pause ever so briefly, touched by
the genuine feeling my outburst had conveyed.

"I'm not interested in any ancient mythology, Barbara, about
your Greeks and Romans, so don't bother telling me that our
bodies are just atoms to be recombined into stars. We've had that
discussion. And as for your island Indians, in my day the Indians
were heathens to be converted, and I haven't much changed my
mind about that. Both Edwin and I arranged our wills so much
of our money goes to seminaries and missions with the rest to
various charities. Do you know, Barbara, that all my medical benefits have run out now for those PUVA treatments. Each one
costs thousands of dollars—right out of my bank account."

"You still have plenty of money, Eloise. You could pay for the
treatments yourself for years and still have money left over."

"But why? I have no other legacy, no children to carry on
good works. I have only the money to leave behind. I can't buy

back youth. I can't buy back health. I can barely see, barely walk, and now I can't drive . . . I have lived a full and, aside from a few youthful indiscretions, upright life. My money can be used in more beneficial ways."

"Have you left money to the church?" I meant the Scotch Grove Presbyterian Church, and I knew there had been arguments with her husband about it. Why did I care so much what happened to that little wooden building on the prairie when I no longer could be counted among those who believed?

"Only a small amount. That church will close in another generation. Edwin said so time and time again."

"It is the oldest church in the county and even if it closed, the building could become some sort of historical museum if you left them money to do that—a testimonial to your ancestors, Eloise, the Sutherlands who came from northern Scotland. You know, Faith of Our Fathers, living still." I tried to inject a lighter note.

"I am not interested, Barbara, in museums, but in promoting a living faith. The seminaries for the future of the faith are better choices."

Eloise paused now before turning the conversation because money had been a touchy subject between us. "And now, Barbara, I must tell you, I have gone against my promise, and I have included in the will a small fund for you."

"Eloise, I—"

"No, Barbara, it is not much. The money I am assigning for your use is not only for you. When you find your brother, the money is to help you attend to his needs."

"I haven't found him, Eloise, and I'm not actively looking for him. I don't know whether he wants to be found."

"You will find him, and it will be soon, so I will know of it before I die."

It was a hard plane ride home to Portland. Deep as my affection was for Eloise, I could understand her reasoning: not only was she demonstrably ill with myeloid lymphoma, the toll of age had rendered her incapable of any of the activities that had given her pleasure in her life. And there was undeniable truth in what she said—her natural life span had been artificially prolonged by a cocktail of medicines. Technically, I reasoned, Eloise's choice was not suicide, and even if it could be classified as such, it seemed important to remember that in some cultures her choice would have been considered honorable. Not that Eloise with her belief in exclusive Christianity would have validated those cultures with a different approach to God, I thought with sad annoyance.

Once I got home, everything changed.

Listening to the phone message from Marge, my Indiana cousin, I felt the room whirl. She had left the number of a Florida nursing home. After I had talked with the woman who headed my brother's care team and decided that the situation demanded that I go to Florida to see him and try to understand his circumstances, I called Eloise.

"Was that just a lucky guess, Eloise, or do you have some kind of inside communication with God?"

Eloise laughed, a dry, cracked sound. She must remember to keep drinking water to keep this ordeal from being unnecessarily uncomfortable. How long would it take to die?

"I prayed, Barbara. Prayer is our inside communication with God. Now you will go and see him. It is a miracle for me that this has happened before I die. If you believe in miracles they will happen, you know. Do you believe in miracles?"

"Probably not the same kind you do, but we've all heard stories of coincidences that are so unusual that they seem miraculous. Yes, I sort of believe in miracles." I thought of what I had written on the beach just a week ago. So this was not really a miracle but certainly not just a coincidence, either. Maybe my scribbled line had been a premonition that my world would tilt, that it was time for the mosaic to change.

For years I did not look for him, and he did not look for me.

Later, on the Nude Beach, I pictured the toy kaleidoscope my brother and I once found under the Christmas tree. The colored pieces in the end of the tube shifted; their sharp edges collided in my brain, and the fragile equilibrium I had established to keep my familial responsibilities at bay dissolved.

෧

The plane did not leave for Orlando until nearly midnight. With the necessary change in Houston, I would not arrive until after daylight, so it was mostly a night of no real sleep, travelling from the northwest corner of the contiguous United States to the southeastern point in Florida. I did not want to think about what I would find, so I concentrated on childhood images of my brother with dark hair and clear blue eyes. He was a handsome boy, others said so. Why Kate, what a handsome young man your Bobbie is becoming. Then I heard the whisper, not Eloise but another woman in the church.

How like his father he looks.

When I first saw my brother I was absolutely positive the curled body in the bed was not his. Someone must have stolen his identity, I thought, during the time he was drinking heavily and surely sleeping on the streets. But his hair was white like mine, and there was something familiar in the way it curved in a slight cowlick on the right side of his forehead. I moved closer and stood by the bed until he opened his eyes and tried to lift himself on one elbow.

"Hello, Barbara," he said.

"Too long."

He fell back on the bed. "Too long," he repeated. "You've been gone too long . . ."

This morning walking on the Nude Beach I could hear the cranes, calling to each other in the clouds, flying back and forth across the river, but at first I could not see them.

Robert, the nurse said as he fell back on the pillow. She shook him gently. Robert, you need to wake up now; your sister is here. I told you she was coming. Not now, he replied, turning his face away from both of us. Tell her to come back later. I need to sleep. So we left the room, and the nurse sat me down in the conference room. He has only come from the hospital yesterday, the nurse named Kellie assured me diplomatically, and he's had sleeping medicine. He'll wake up in a little while, and you can talk with him then. He never mentioned any family at all. How did you find him?

That was better. I could talk to the nurse about factual things as we sat in the conference room and, gaining my composure, I said I had a call from my cousin Marge, the self-appointed family historian. Marge had sent materials for a family reunion with her own phone number on them to his last known address, which had eventually reached his ex-wife Karen, who had forwarded the reunion materials to him. Karen had kept track of him because of their children, and I had always known if I wanted to find him that I could call her. Cousin Marge, who somehow knew the family reunion materials reached him, told me that she had kept sporadically in touch with Bobbie, Marge used the childhood name, by sending fruit baskets on special occasions—she did that for all the members of the family who were ill.

I had always known I could find him, I repeated in a garbled apology to a nurse who had no real interest in either my brother or me and was only being polite, through either Marge or his ex-wife Karen, but I wasn't at all sure he wanted to be found.

Do come back a little later, the nurse said soothingly. Robert will wake up and perhaps his mind will be clear. Sometimes he sounds quite intelligent and seems to know everything that is going on around him. Tomorrow he may feel somewhat stronger, and you can take him for a short ride in the afternoon. No more than three or four hours as he is incontinent now, you know, and cannot control his systems.

So I left then, and sat in the rental car in the nursing home parking lot. After I got control of my voice, I called Eloise.

"How are you feeling, Eloise?"

"I am feeling fine, Barbara, only a little tired. This would go faster if I could keep from eating anything but my body resists that. Did you find him? Are you there with him?"

Her voice was always husky now, as if she could not quite clear her throat.

"Yes, he is sleeping now."

"Did he know you? What did he say when he saw you?"

"He said I'd been gone too long."

I thought, but did not say to Eloise, that I had felt a surprising and confusing surge of rage at that. *Too long?* I wanted to scream at him. *I've* been gone too long? *I'm* not the one who lost our mother's farm, who left my children behind, who gave over my life to alcohol. What do you mean *I've* been gone?

"How did he look?" Eloise asked huskily.

"Terrible. He weighs only 112 pounds, according to the nurse. Eloise, he was six foot two when I knew him. His legs protruded from the sheets and the bones were like those concentration camp pictures. He cannot straighten them at all due to some spinal curvature and muscle deterioration. Eloise, I'm not sure this was such a good idea."

I was trying not to cry.

"But he knew you?"

"Yes. He said, hello, Barbara. He said, you've been gone too long. Eloise, they call him Robert in this nursing home. We never called him Robert."

"Of course they call him Robert," Eloise said. "Some of us did, too, after he was grown. Your grandmother in Minnesota did and I did, too, when we visited, and he was there."

When I came home to Oregon, among all the sad things from my visit, it was the look of those concentration-camp legs, the skeletal bones, that I could not get out of my mind. I was glad to be back on the island, but I could not sleep that night, thinking of things I had heard and read.

A year or so ago I talked with the elderly woman who lives at the farmstead that covers the Cath-lah-min-na-min site, one of the largest island villages that was just a mile or so downstream from our houseboat. She told me that a long time ago, maybe during the sixties, when she and her husband let the Oregon Archeological Society dig in their front yard, all the bones of the natives who died so quickly in the Great Pestilence were put in one of the buildings on their property for temporary storage. "I had to call the leader," she said, "the man who was in charge of the dig, because the dogs were dragging the bones from the shed."

❧

There were people to tell. I called Eloise every day now, even though she did not make much sense on the phone, and the Minnesota cousin was staying with her. "You will have to come soon," the Minnesota cousin said. "Mostly she just sleeps."

"Has she asked more about my brother? She had been so insistent that I go and find him."

"No," said the Minnesota cousin. "I guess that is settled now. It is the ones of her own generation that she seems to be talking to. I'm coming, Robert; I'm coming, Wilma, she says, almost like she is singing. By the way, what's with the song about the river?"

There were others who would want to know. Cousin Marge, whose card for the family reunion had found him and who sent the fruit baskets. She had been given the address of the nursing home when she had been called about an infection Bobbie had contracted.

"Did you take a picture?" Marge wanted pictures to put on a board at the family reunions. "Did you meet the woman named Tami? A woman named Tami called here once, and I can give you her number."

"No, but he spoke of her. 'Next time you come you must meet Tami,' he said. "She is so beautiful. Tami and Gary. I lived with their family for sixteen years.'"

"I'll do that, Bobbie," I had said to him, stroking his hair before I left. I did not say that I could have come back to see him in the morning before my plane returned to Portland but would not do so because my chest hurt to even think of it.

"Did you take a picture?" Marge was insistent about this. "Why didn't you take a picture? I'd like to see a picture of him. Take a picture of Tami, too."

"Maybe next time, Marge." Don't wait so long, he had said. "I'll go again in a couple of months."

If he's still alive, I thought. It had simply never occurred to me to take a picture of my brother in that sorry condition.

Then Vaneta. *We all loved him once.*

"Thank you for your love and concern, Vaneta. Both, believe me, were needed." Then I proceeded to describe to my cousin in great detail the shock and dismay I had felt at seeing my brother that way, curled into almost a fetal position; the severe thunderstorm that had forced me to pull to the side of the road on the way back from Daytona Beach, how I had wanted to say do you remember the time we were down at the big tree at the end of the field, and the thunder came, and we huddled . . . but he was asleep with his body slumped in an unbelievably contorted position, and for all the crashing and the rain drumming like marbles on the roof of the rented car he did not wake up. How the motel that sounded okay on the Internet had been such a dump, right next to the Straight Shoot Range, and the first night I stayed there, at one o'clock in the morning bullets were still going ka-thunk, ka-thunk, ka-thunk.

"But aren't you glad, Barb, that you have finally found him? Don't you think your mother would be pleased?"

"I guess so, Vaneta."

When they took him from the car—it took three nurse's aides, and they had to call one of the men because my brother was in such a contorted position—they put him in a wheelchair. Turn the chair, he said, turn the chair so I can see her go. So they did, and he tried to wave. Come back soon, he said. Don't wait so long. When I left, the rain began and again I had to pull to the side of the highway until it lessened. How nature mocks us with overworked metaphors, I thought cynically. I drove back out to Leesburg because I didn't want to listen to the guns at the Straight Shoot Range. By that time the thunderstorm had blown completely away.

Now there was only Karen, Bob's ex-wife, who had been helpful before when approached directly. I wanted addresses for my nephews as it was surely time to rectify some of my own neglect as an aunt. That could wait until morning, I decided, leaning against the window for the coolness on my forehead. Perhaps e-mail would be better for that conversation. No moon bobbed on the river, but the customary evening calm had not settled on the water, and occasional rain fluttered against the glass. Thank god the coyotes were quiet. I did not re-read any of the last notebook entries I had written, especially the one I had transcribed on the way to Florida. I had not slept well for several nights, and I was already feeling unable to change sad things.

Last week as I looked up from my work, a deer emerged from the bushes that line the shore on the other side of the water. It looked around carefully before it lowered its head to drink. I turned back to my work—then heard a wild shriek. Two coyotes leapt from the bushes and took that deer down right in front of my eyes. The dogs, who had been watching the deer from the lower deck, pressed to the railing in silent, rapt attention.

I couldn't look and couldn't look away, but an old piling standing in the middle of the creek bed where the deer had walked out hid some of the grisly scene from my view. The long deer legs twitched; the coyotes lifted their heads and stared across the river at the dogs. I ran downstairs and pulled the dogs inside, but the coyotes had drawn back into the bushes. Please let the deer be dead, I prayed, and I went back upstairs and looked through my binoculars.

It wasn't dead. At first it just twitched and thrashed around; then it lurched to its feet and fell again. Probably the coyotes had cut a tendon. It lurched again, this time actually managing to get up on the belt of grass behind the mud. There it sat down like a fawn, its head nervously jerking from side to side. It sat there the rest of the day. I wanted to lower the shade but I didn't. Both the deer and I knew for sure the coyotes were just back in the bushes waiting, because they howled when a siren went by on the island dike road.

Thank god there were errands I had to run and of course the dogs had to be walked. Each time I came back I looked again and the deer was still there, watching. Once I thought it was gone, but it had just slid farther back in the grass. It couldn't run, and I knew it. Just before it got too dark I looked again, and it was still there. I pulled my pillow around my ears when I went to bed because I didn't want to hear the coyotes yammering as they fed their young.

ᗝ

On the second day of the visit to Orlando, the nurses had arranged for me to take my brother for a ride, and when I arrived they had him in a wheelchair. He wanted to go to Daytona Beach, and when we got on the freeway, he was surprisingly alert, giving directions and a commentary on the surrounding geography. I asked no questions about his past, but he volunteered that he had lived in Florida since around 1980 and that he had worked at a citrus plant. He did not glance sideways or meet my eyes, and most of the time he talked to me as if I were a stranger, saying things like my mother used to say this or that without any acknowledgement that we shared the same mother, so I wasn't always sure that he knew who I was.

He seemed to remember the relatives and asked specifically about Vaneta and Eloise. Eloise was not well; in fact she may die soon, I told him, but I did not explain. You'd better go see her then, he said. I could give you the money to go see her, he said, although I already knew that he did not have any money. Robert was always giving it away to the nursing home help, I was told, so they had to lock up the thirty-five dollars he was allowed to keep each month from his social security check. He remembered the exact roads, turns, back lanes to Daytona Beach, and after I had driven around the empty stadium he directed me to the beach and for five dollars we drove right down on the sand itself. The incoming waves were small and quiet, nothing like the Pacific. He knew where to stop to get an ice cream cone. I was in tears trying to clean up the ensuing disaster due to his worthless hands, which were stiffened into claws. That night the bullets still beat an erratic rhythm at the Straight Shoot Range, and I could not sleep, so I wrote for a while instead.

When we were kids on the farm, we had only the small Frigidaire that sat on the open back porch, exposed to the elements. Grandma still called it the icebox, but the small freezing compartment barely made ice cubes and certainly did not keep ice cream frozen. In summer, if we had been quiet and polite in Long's Grocery, if we had not run in the frozen arctic aisles of the meat locker where our mother picked up neatly wrapped brown packages for the week, we could have an ice cream cone on the way home. We licked carefully at the edges because we must never, ever let the ice cream drip on the dusty plush seats of the 1940 Ford. This is not really our car, our mother said. Our car is gone. This car belonged to my father.

Why are you crying, Bobbie asked me when I mopped furiously at the ice cream dripping from his crippled hands. This is not really our car.

"And now you have found your brother, and I have a strange feeling that I will find mine as well," said Madeline the next time we went to the John Street Café.

"Are you looking for him?"

"Definitely not. You weren't exactly looking for yours, either."

She called that right, for sure. We waited silently while the waitress delivered our order.

"All families have alcoholics," said Madeline. "Ask anybody, and they have an alcoholic relative story." That was certainly true.

I'm glad my mother never knew about Bobbie's drinking—that was a sin in the church and in our family for sure. When she died he was in the army, stationed in England, and she was proud of that. She wouldn't have been able to handle the fact that he was an alcoholic.

"I can't bear any more shame, Barbie" (*Prairie Reunion*, 261).

"It was that DUI that threw my brother into a tailspin. That's when he totally disappeared." That was Madeline speaking, but it could have been me, I thought, remembering Eloise's words about Bobbie's downhill slide. I asked again whether Madeline had totally forgotten about her brother for long stretches like I had done with Bobbie. This weighed heavily on me now, especially that he was in such a weakened condition.

"I was used to my brother being gone for long periods of time after all those times he went on the lam, and then finally he would show up again," said Madeline. "If someone who knew us as children inquired about him, I'd say, 'He's lost. A homeless guy. We don't know where he is, or even if he's alive.'"

A homeless guy. Well, yes, I had said something like that about Bobbie. It's like he's already dead for me, I'd told relatives when they expressed wonderment that I had totally lost touch with him. I grieved and worried for years, but now it's like he's already dead. But it wasn't really quite like that, and he wasn't already dead.

❧

"The interment for Eloise was like the opening scene in *Doctor Zhivago*," I wrote to my brother as if he had gone to the movies like the rest of us instead of being god knows where on the street, "with the little kid standing by the grave, and the wind whipping snow across the steppe. I had forgotten that Iowa could be so cold."

It took Eloise more than a few weeks to die. In the meantime, flying back and forth from Oregon to Arizona, I wrote letters to my brother about Eloise's condition as if he could read them, but when I went to Florida again I found them unopened in the nightstand by his bed. Did the nurse not realize that he couldn't open them himself, or had he told her to put them there and forgotten about them? Maybe, I thought suddenly, he didn't *want* to read them. I addressed him as if he were perfectly normal, at least mentally, when I hadn't a clue what was going on in his mind. "Eloise has given over a million dollars for a new regional hospital in Jones County, Bobbie. She used the money from the sale of the ancestral Sutherland land. Some children in the community wrote thank-you notes for her gift, and the last time she was really coherent they had just arrived by express mail. In a show of strength and clarity that surprised us all, Eloise sat up in bed and asked me to put her glasses on her face. I read the notes to her and showed her the pictures the children had drawn: flowers, birds, trees, and little animals. Eloise even managed to smile at the notes, which was amazing as she had been incoherent and mostly unconscious all the previous day. You must have a lot of money, said one. It is a good thing to have a nice place to be sick in a new hospital, said another. You must be a very, very, very nice lady, said the one that Eloise reached out for, and when I put it in her hand, she held the card against her heart."

When Eloise had fallen into what the doctor assured me would be the final coma, I kept my plane reservation and flew home. The next day the Minnesota cousin called.

"It was a touching scene when she finally slipped away, Barb. All the old gals who had known her on the third floor of the residence hall came in and surrounded the bed. They held hands and said the Lord's Prayer together and stood there, swaying back and forth. They are probably, every one of them, over ninety, and I think most would have been only too glad to jump in the boat with her and cross that river she kept singing about. I was afraid they all were going to fall over, and I'd have to carry them out."

I did have to cancel the Florida trip I had planned in order to tend to the memorial service for Eloise in Iowa, which meant I would not be going to see Bobbie again until after Christmas. I tried to call, but as there was no phone service in his room, the call had to be carefully coordinated with the nursing station. The next day when I tried again, the nurse said the battery on the handset had been all run down by another patient, and they only had one phone on that floor so I'd have to wait until it recharged. After three days of trying each morning, I gave it up and wrote another letter instead, but of course he couldn't open it to read it. He hadn't read the one I sent after Eloise's service either.

"The service was at the Sandhill Church, Bobbie, and that is where Edwin's had been, too. Her only stipulation had been that she wanted her service just a little bigger and better than Edwin's. They argued about which cemetery to use—Edwin had grown up Lutheran, you know, and didn't want to be buried with the Presbyterians. They ended up compromising by buying a lot in the Monticello Cemetery because it is nondenominational, and Edwin thought it was the most likely to have the weeds mowed. I promised Eloise I would put an inscription for her on one of the family stones at the Scotch Grove cemetery, either Clark or Sutherland, so anyone doing genealogical research could find a reference to her in Scotch Grove. That will have to wait for spring. I was disappointed that we could not hold the memorial service at our old church. She was so proud of the fact that her Sutherland ancestors from Scotland had founded it and that she had been the first woman elder who had been allowed to serve. It was bitterly cold in Iowa, and it takes days to warm up even the sanctuary so I didn't think I could insist that we hold the service there and have all those old people sit there shivering. Eloise had asked me some time ago to give the eulogy, so I did. I started this way: If there are cars in heaven, I hope God lets Eloise drive one and lets her drive it fast.

"Already I miss her terribly, Bobbie. Isn't it odd how we never referred to her as a relative at all when we children? Lately, I have grown to love her almost as much as I loved our mother.

"After the service those who could stand the cold went to the Monticello Cemetery some five miles away from the Sand-hill Church. Now that you're living in sunny Florida, Bobbie, you may have forgotten what an extremely grim place Iowa can be in the winter and how cold it was in the upstairs bedrooms. After Eloise's funeral I went to the Scotch Grove cemetery to find Paul Ernie's grave. The snow was over my boots, and I had left my heavy coat in the car. I felt like a lonely child with so many neighbors and friends from the church already dead, the snow swirling around their stones. I went back to Grandma's house to stay with Vaneta, and I slept in Mom's room. All night the tree limbs tossed and cracked in the subzero temperatures."

I first asked my brother if he would like to come to an Oregon nursing home in a letter, but I asked him again when I next saw him face to face, and I meant it. Eloise had given me the money to make that happen. Do what you have to do, my husband had said. You've spent way too long feeling guilty about this, and we'll work it out somehow if he says he wants to come.

I could see you often, I said to my brother, and bring you to the houseboat for the day. It's beautiful where I live. How I would ever get a wheelchair down the ramp I did not know, but I didn't mention that. He leaned his head to one side as if not entirely sure what I was offering. I repeated the question again. In the letter I had pleaded the case eloquently, but when I saw him in person, I was momentarily terrified that he might say yes.

Are you out of your *mind,* my cousin Vaneta had demanded when I was back for Eloise's service and mentioned I was trying to do this. Vaneta reinforced her opinion with e-mails later. Don't do it, Barb. I absolutely insist that you don't put this on yourself. Think of your husband. I don't care how much money Eloise left you for this, the money would run out in a hurry. Do NOT even think about it.

Vaneta, it was your idea that I had to find him, I e-mailed in return. You and Eloise. How did you expect me to feel when I found him in such a sorry condition? Just in case there is really a heaven, I do not want to meet my mother and say I not only neglected my brother for thirty years, but once I finally found him I left him to die alone in Florida. Let this be a cautionary tale for those who try to redeem their guilt at the end of improvident relatives' lives.

So I did think about bringing him to Oregon, and just for a minute I thought it might turn out that way. The implications of the expensive medical journey it would require, the possibility that I might actually endanger our financial future, the difficulty of making the complicated arrangements seemed overwhelming, but I repeated the offer when I saw my brother in person the second time. If not Oregon, would he like to return to Iowa, where he could be close to his sons? By then I was in contact with them and that had been suggested.

My brother stared at me for so long that I wondered if he was seriously considering the move or whether his undependable lucidity had already slipped away. Just before he lapsed into sleep he gave his answer, in a surprisingly strong voice. "No. I've never lived in Oregon, so it is not my home," he said clearly, "and Iowa is too cold."

Do you remember, Bobbie, what it was like the night when Mom died? It was the twelfth of December with a full moon, and you had come home from England where you were stationed at Harrogate. The temperature was twelve degrees below zero.

A wave of guilty relief swept through me when he said he wouldn't come, and it swept through me again when the dogs frolicked in front of me on the beach, Devi in and out of the water and Pani barking and barking, intent on dislodging a heron from its perch on a piling. Finally the heron flew away with a croak that sounded like my brother coughing. In my heart I knew all along he would not come, and it made me feel a little ashamed that I had gone through this charade, so I tried not to think about it.

The wind helped.

⌒

Even though Eloise was safely dispatched to heaven, I still had my brother to deal with, so the Nude Beach became more of a sanctuary than ever, a place to get my thoughts in order. I walked more slowly than usual along the edge of the water. The January day was cold with a sharp wind, and in the morning the dark sand where the tide had receded broke in large slabs like a shattered chocolate bar. The dogs loved it and raced around wildly. This was the weather they were made for, and they knew it. In the afternoon the sand had softened slightly, but it was still cold, very cold for Portland, with a weak sun low in the southern sky. Pani carried a chunk of ice-foam like a prize, and Devi came out of the water with tinseled frozen fur.

Could it be, I found myself thinking as I walked on the pliant sand, that Eloise was really in heaven now because she believed it was there? I'd have to discuss this with Madeline; certainly my husband didn't want to talk about it. You can believe in it all you want, he said, but if it's not there, it's not there.

But belief was a powerful thing; I'd seen it in action, not just with my Christian relatives, but with my friend Jan, who studied shaman rituals. Jan could walk over hot coals in her bare feet. You have to have faith in your ability to do it, Jan said; if you believe, all sorts of miracles are possible. Marilyn did it, Barb, Jan said, referring to a mutual friend to whom we both gave great credit for spirituality, and you can, too.

All of this began with a course about miracles Jan studied that incorporated traditional Christianity in a transformative spiritual experience involving spirits and guides. The next year Jan was among a group of women I had taken to Nepal, and sure enough, Jan was the one who made it up Kala Patar to see that black Everest face while the rest of us went back down to the medical station at Pheriche with various illnesses. You have to believe it will happen, Jan explained, her face radiating with joyful confidence. You have to believe that the clouds will part, and they do. With further study Jan had become a shaman herself and even started a new church with like-minded people.

Had I become an inveterate unbeliever? Jan's spiritual path had certainly not worked for me. Once, out of curiosity, I had gone with Jan to a sweat lodge where, as we purged ourselves with steam, we were to ask our ancestors for guidance. Which ancestors, I had queried skeptically. Some of mine had rather lousy judgment, and I didn't want to pray to them. I had honestly thought I might die, stretched out on the damp earthen floor as I tried to suck in what little air still hovered beneath the steam. Was it because I didn't believe that this sweat lodge ceremony was such a miserable experience? Had I tried to walk on hot coals I would have severely burned my feet.

We are given eternal life because we believe, Eloise had told me, and because we have faith. "Faith is the substance of things hoped for, the evidence of things not seen" (Hebrews 11:1). "He that cometh to God must believe that he is . . . and that he is a rewarder of them that diligently seek him" (Hebrews 11: 6).

"Help thou my unbelief," I had said with an unfortunate lilt, because I wanted to change the subject, and Eloise had scolded me, saying that I must not mock religion; whatever would my mother and my Sunday school teacher Ella Clark think? The first part of that verse, which had to do with Jesus casting out a child's epilepsy, went like this: "And straightway the father of the child cried out and said with tears, Lord I believe; help thou mine unbelief" (Matthew 9:24). I'll pray for your soul, Barbara, Eloise said sharply, and that was the end of that.

So what a surprise to find that my nephew, my brother's son, the one with the unfortunate family name of Robert, was on Eloise's wavelength about God.

"What color is your hair?" I had asked that in the first phone call.

"It's almost white already, like yours was at that book reading." That was the only time he had seen me, when his mother had taken him to the reading at Sweet Memories Bed and Breakfast to prove to him that there was more on his father's side of the family than just alcoholism. Now he was almost forty.

"And your eyes?"

"Blue."

"What name do you go by?"

"Bob," he said. "I go by Bob, Aunt Barbara. I have been blessed with a lovely wife named Stacie and two beautiful children, Ben and Rachel. I work for the State of Iowa in computer programing, and I live in Des Moines. I can't believe I'm finally talking to you. I've thought of it many times, and now it's almost a surreal experience."

It was more of a nervous experience for me than a surreal one, and the appellative he had used, Aunt Barbara, strangely shocked me. I had been a lousy aunt, and I knew it. Was there a Biblical injunction I had missed about that particular duty? I was now anxious to atone for my sins. I was glad he did not call himself Robert. "I need to speak with you about your father," I had said, and we talked for a long time. He and his brother had counseling about chemical abuse and addiction when they were young, he said, and it had helped him immensely to be nonjudgmental about his parents. After this contact he was thinking that perhaps he would discuss with his wife the possibility of taking the family to Florida to see his father.

My nephew Bob had sounded so well adjusted and happy, and he said his brother, Bill, was equally settled—a family man with two teenagers, a trucker who had driven his own rig for years but now worked in the main office. How could this be, this miracle of stability and traditional values, when these boys had an alcoholic father and a mother with drug problems? True, they had been mostly raised by the maternal grandparents, but they had high odds against them genetically for turning out so well. Was it the counseling they had received or just their own resilience?

God, Eloise would have said.

"Is your brother religious, too?" I had asked. "Did your grandparents take you to church?"

"Not so much," he had answered to both questions, "but I came to religion mostly on my own. Bill came to his when he was laid up with vertigo and couldn't work for two years."

What a strange world, I thought as I tightened my hood against the wind. The cold beach was predictably unpopulated this afternoon. There seemed to me to be no rational explanations for most of what I encountered, most recently the surprising goodness and success in life of my brother's sons. At the moment, if given a multiple-choice list of the possibilities, I would certainly select the chaos view of the universe.

"Part of accepting God's grace is to believe that Jesus is who He said He is—God's son, and to enter into a relationship with Him," my nephew had said in one of our e-mail exchanges. "I would love to have more dialogue with you on questions of faith."

My mind jumped to the kind of dialogues I had with Eloise in the decade we had been so close. They had strained the very basis of our relationship. Many during that historical time period, even before and after, claimed to be sons of various gods, I had reminded Eloise. Consider Mithraism. There were a raft of mystery religions in the Middle East, I wanted to say now to my nephew, but I didn't. I didn't want to argue with my brother's son. I was so glad to discover him and his brother. I didn't want to discuss God, either. I was not unhappy with my spiritual state of mind, so why were the relatives? Could we talk about other things, I asked silently, and my nephew sensed my reserve, so we did. It turned out we both liked birds, so mostly we talked about that and other aspects of nature, and about my brother, too, of course. Whenever his son brought up religion, I deflected with general answers.

More than anything right now I wanted this young man to love and respect me. He and his brother offered an unexpected ray of hope; they might yet provide some redemption to my brother's mostly wasted existence. But I was not going to lie about religion or pretend that I still believed in the exclusivity of Christianity. It had done too much damage for that, even when there was an underlying similarity of belief like the surprising parallel I had found in last winter's reading.

Franchere was told by a son of Chief Concomly that the natives on the lower Columbia believed in a divinity named Etalapass, the creator, and another slightly lesser one, perhaps his son, called Ecannum who was of a more human bent. He gave people sight and taught them speech. From Ecannum they learned all practical building tasks, such as how to make their canoes, and all the skills related to catching fish, such as constructing their complicated nets and weirs and their strong fishing lines made of nettles.

☙

The very next day I saw the Naked-Red-Girl with her boa on the beach. The snow had come during the night, silently stacking itself on the railing to a height of about four inches, and the dogs were so excited when they discovered it, I was afraid they would fall off the deck wrestling with each other. We arrived at the Nude Beach just as the sun was cresting the clouds that were moving toward Mount Hood in the east. The sand where the tide had receded was not entirely frozen, and it bent like heavy felt under my boots. The dogs ran circles like children, scattering the snow in scarlet feathers.

I had almost reached the End of the Nude Beach sign when I saw the Naked-Red-Girl. Always before I had seen this woman posing in warmer weather, but now, obviously enthralled with the contrast of the snow-covered logs and her rosy skin, the photographer was positioning and re-positioning the woman to find the correct lighting. The Naked-Red-Girl, whose only adornment was a feathered red boa, moved in wooden response, no doubt already numb with cold.

I stared in disbelief at what this man was asking the girl to do in such inclement conditions, and the dogs stood momentarily silent beside me. Take off your own coat, I thought of screaming at the well-clothed photographer. If you're going to freeze her limbs for the sake of your pornographic pictures, you should suffer as well. The woman, who seemed not at all the young girl I had previously imagined, but well on the far edge of youth, turned large eyes framed by exaggerated eyelashes my way and held up her hand as if to stop me from saying anything. I need the money, she seemed to be pleading; please don't interfere. In a few minutes they ended the photographic session, and the Naked-Red-Girl, who did not look my way again, wrapped a large blanket around her body, and the strange couple disappeared down the transvestite path through the trees.

The dogs went back to their furious frolic along the snow-covered sand, and I turned around at the End of the Nude Beach sign. What a strange world, I thought, in an echo of yesterday's musings about religion, and we mostly make sense of it by imposing our own value system on what we see. Had this been a child who was nude in the snow there would be a reason to report the episode to the authorities. This girl is being exploited, I could have insisted, and you need to track down this crazy man who is subjecting her to frostbite, hypothermia, and unnecessarily endangering her health. And had indeed a child been involved, authorities might have been willing to intervene, but the Naked-Red-Girl seemed at least a consenting not-so-young participant in this seemingly senseless exercise. I could relate to that. "Why are you still climbing those ridiculous mountains," Eloise had repeatedly demanded. "I absolutely insist that you give it up. You'll get frostbite; even worse, hypothermia. At your age you ought to have more sense than to endanger your health." At least I had never climbed a mountain without my clothes.

I was making that up about the woman needing money, I thought as I drove back to the moorage. Maybe the Naked-Red-Girl was like Candy, the woman I heard about when we first moved to the moorage, the one who had jumped nude from her houseboat roof into the river. According to the eighty-year-old woman who got hauled off because her kids suspected Alzheimer's, Candy had grown up in one of Portland's priciest suburbs. She wasn't abused, so the story went; she took to the streets as a prostitute by choice because she couldn't stand the social culture of her parents, and after she perfected her trade, she became a madam. "Candy was an extremely intelligent woman," insisted Julia, who had lived for seventeen years at the upstream end of the moorage. "And she didn't jump nude from the roof, she jumped from the deck. Actually the story was that when she had parties, she stripped off her clothes in the house and ran nude through the party guests on the deck to dive into the river. She wrote a book on how to be a successful madam. We all wanted to read it, but when someone finally got a copy, we found it wasn't racy at all, just about cleanliness and avoiding disease and taking good care of her girls. Candy told me once that she reviewed books for the library. I figured she meant cheap romances, but she showed me one that had just come in the mail: *In My Place*, the

autobiography of Charlayne Hunter-Gault, a reporter and com-
mentator for public broadcasting." Candy even plied her trade for
a few years at the moorage, Mike Denny had said. By his account,
a tugboat would pull up at her houseboat and after a while the
pilot would get back in the boat with a smile on his face.

I pulled into our parking lot with a sudden new appreciation
for our little moorage and its idiosyncrasies. Even a few decades
ago, houseboat living was mostly for those who could not afford
to live anywhere else, those on the fringe of respectability, the
social cast-offs and the misunderstood. Often the houseboats
were no more than a single-wide trailer on a raft. Now there were
several moorages that had become quite as upscale as gated com-
munities with expensive fees. Not our moorage; it was still com-
fortably informal with a mixture of houses and people, and Jim
and I were glad for that. Mike Denny told us when we first came
that Mayfair had once been one of the scruffiest moorages on the
river with quite a reputation for derelicts. "We used to have some
pretty interesting people here," he said. Then he laughed. "You
look a little too respectable, but I guess we'll let you in."

◯

After a couple more visits to Florida and several phone calls,
I had managed to schedule all the members of my brother's care
team at the nursing home for a meeting to apprise me of exactly
what the medical problems were and how I could possibly assist
in his care even though I lived in Oregon. The meeting was
attended by the unit manager, the care plan manager, the dietary
manager, the rehab manager, the fill-in social worker (the usual
one was on maternity leave), and a woman named Sherrie who
worked in a department called "restorative." It turned out, after
several loud calls over the intercom to get the last member of the
team to the meeting, that the nurse had forgotten to have my

brother sign the permission form that was needed for them to release any information to me.

"He is his own man, you know, and has not given permission for anyone to share his medical records," the care plan manager said rather tartly.

"His own man?" Was that a medical designation? A man who was bedridden and had been described to me as psychotic was deemed mentally competent to refuse any physical therapy to keep his muscles working? "Please get the form signed right now," I demanded, "as I have finally managed to get you all together so we know where the contradictions in information I have been getting are coming from. I am going back to Oregon tomorrow so this has to happen now." It was beginning to look like I might have to psychically block the door as they were all offering excuses as to why they needed to leave in a minute or two. Moved by the dangerously sharp edge to my voice, the nurse went out and returned promptly with a form that had a totally illegible scrawl at the bottom.

The staff was not really hostile, just overworked and hot, too many of them crowded into this office because the conference room was occupied and they couldn't use it, I told my husband later when I called. "I'm beginning to think, however, that Tami has been right that he has suffered from borderline neglect." I had finally met Tami the night before and taken her and her husband Gary to dinner. Tami had chosen the Olive Garden, and the couple ate a lot, asking for boxes for leftovers, even the crackers and bread.

"They don't pay no attention to me when I complain about his sores," Tami said. "I'm up there every two weeks or so, but I never sign in, I just walk right past the desk and they don't say nothin'. They say I have nothin' to say about what happens even when I can see that they haven't been tending to him because I'm not family. Bob lived with us for sixteen years, and my kids loved him. They still call him Uncle Bob. We didn't even know that you even existed so if we ain't family, I don't know who is. Almost every time I go to see him he remembers a little wind-up chicken that came in one of those fruit baskets that Marge sent. Make the little chicken dance, Tami, he says, and I put it on his tray-table and wind it up. That silly little chicken bounces all over the place, sometimes hopping from the table to the bed, and he laughs out loud and calls for the nurse to watch."

Tami, to her credit, did not once refer to my brother as Robert. She was plump, blond, about forty-five, and, as my brother had said, quite pretty. Tami worked at the telephone company, and Gary didn't work anymore because he hurt his back in some sort of construction accident. I was never able to quite figure out my brother's relationship with this family, although Tami and I had many phone conversations about my brother's health, and it was obvious that she cared about him deeply. "It started out that he lived next door," she said, "but the house was sold, and he had no place else to go so he stayed with us for a few days. Somehow that turned into sixteen years," she continued with a smile. "He helped so much with our children." *But what about his own*, I thought in anguish the night when she told me this.

"Here's what's wrong with your father," I wrote in an e-mail later to his sons. "I don't know what, if any of this, is a result of the drinking or whether it's mostly age and neglect. I'm typing from a doctor's report, a report that was voluminous, but they charged me a ridiculous ten dollars a page to copy it. Are you sure you don't mean ten cents a page? I demanded. How could it cost ten dollars a page? But the aide could not find anyone who knew, so I had to pay the money in cash, and I ended up copying only ten pages. He has Renal Failure, Esophageal Reflux, Peptic Ulcer Disease, Mental Disease, Peripheral Vascular Disease, Anxiety, Unspecified Psychoses, Cervical Spondylosis, Benign Prostatic Hypertrophy, Myelopathy, and another report mentions depression and aggressive tendencies. A mysterious hospital admission from last year mentions dementia, that he was 'uncompliant,' refused tests, and I quote from the doctor who made the entry:

'He even struck me as I was trying to examine him,' and the following, that I find unbelievable. 'I discussed this with the patient's family, and they state that the patient is known to be belligerent.'"

"Exactly what is mental disease," I complained to Jim later on the phone. "Or unspecified psychoses? Did he pickle his brain with alcohol or is this some genetic-oriented problem? I suppose there is no impetus on their part to determine exactly what is wrong with his mind as there has been no one to report to. It is easier for them to just call everything dementia."

I ran the meeting with the nursing home staff myself. I asked for a story or an anecdote from each one of them that would illustrate something about this man of whom I knew so little. This seemed to be difficult for all of them, and they often looked at each other as if they were asking for help. Was that Robert or was that Edgar or Mr. Johnson, they asked each other, and twice said things like I have only been here two months so actually, I haven't seen him much. The general tenor of their somewhat fractured picture was that Robert was difficult to work with; that he was unpredictable in his responses; that he seldom joked around anymore, although one of them remembered when he did so; that he was uncooperative with any kind of therapy. "Leave me alone," he had told the rehab manager when he signed a form releasing them from any treatment. "No one cares if I die, anyway."

I asked for a list of his medications, which seemed to be difficult to find. The list they had was mostly abbreviations, and the condition each medication was to alleviate was not specified. Finally someone volunteered that he was on drugs for depression, anxiety, and mineral deficiencies. They needed to keep him quite heavily medicated in case he became uncompliant.

Uncompliant? Was that a medical term like "his own man?"

"How do we know," I asked my husband on the phone, "what is really wrong in his head and what is the result of interacting medications? When he wakes up and hasn't had any pills for a long time, he seems to make quite a bit of sense. His memory of childhood things or of relatives or people we knew as kids is quite amazing then."

"We never knew how he ended up in Florida," Tami said. "We knew he came from Iowa and that his grandfather once had a lot of land. That land was a big deal for him, we knew that. That was the only family he talked about. He would look after my kids until we got off work. His back was already bad then, and he said it was a tennis injury. We was awfully fond of Bob, and I woulda kept him in our trailer, but once he couldn't hold his bowels, well, I couldn't handle that. He did just get god-awful drunk when he was younger, though. Once he nearly burned down our trailer when he fell asleep drunk with a cigarette in his hand."

He had done that once before, fallen asleep drunk with a cigarette in his hand, but they always said it was a short in the clock radio by the bed, his ex-wife Karen told me when I specifically asked about the fire. Do you think I could live with that, he had said to Karen, who had left him shortly after that to try to get her own life in order. Do you think I could live thinking that I almost killed my family by burning down the house? "Barbara, he always had the craziest get-rich schemes," Karen told me. "They had no basis in reality, and a shyster could talk him into investing in anything because he was so trusting and honest himself. That got worse when he drank. One time it was raising rabbits. But the rabbits all got cancer, and I can't even talk about that." Not long after I contacted Karen, she wrote a most unusual letter to her ex-husband, the father of her sons, and she sent me a copy.

"When I read that you said no one cares if you live or die, Bob, I was surprised and shocked. Your sons care, your sister cares, and yes, your ex-wife cares what happens to you. Tami and the family that you lived with for so many years care what happens to you.

"Bob, you have two loving sons who have grown up to be successful in life, and you had a part in that despite alcoholism creeping in like a thief in the night to steal your life and family away from you. You supported the boys financially from the sale of your land, and they did not want for anything as far as money was concerned as a result. The boys both married well, and we have four wonderful grandchildren.

"Bob, I know you did not want a divorce. I didn't understand addiction then, but I certainly understand it now. You have so many things to be grateful for, especially the boys and their families and a sister who truly does love you and desperately wants to make up for past neglect. I hope you will give her a chance."

This group of caregivers at the nursing home had obviously reached the end of the line with my brother. When I peppered them with more questions at the meeting—could the list I had finally been shown of his numerous medications possibly contribute to his confused dementia, for example—the unit manager ignored the question and suggested to the others that they might need to get back to their work. She asked whether I would consider putting Robert on hospice, now that I, as his sister, had been given authority to make medical decisions on his behalf.

Hospice? Did that mean that he was expected to die within a few weeks?

Oh, not necessarily, the unit manager said soothingly, rolling her eyes a little and motioning toward the door so the others knew they had permission to leave, which they promptly did in an almost frantic scramble. We have many residents on hospice. Hospice was completely covered for him by his Medicare and Medicaid, now that the bank account he had when he arrived had been fully exhausted. The payments would go directly to the nursing home for room and board, but Robert would qualify for hospice under the general "failure to thrive" category.

"He has a documented weight loss, and we have been unable to get those nasty sores on his hips to respond. Your brother would have extra care because the hospice nurse comes twice a week, and they would bathe him. These federal programs have additional equipment that could be used for rehabilitation. Of course, the patients on hospice have to pass periodic reviews to make sure they still qualify, but they almost always are renewed."

"I can see," I told Jim on the phone, "that this is an advantage for the nursing home anyway, but I agreed to it because I thought any extra care he would get would be worth it. I'm not exactly sure what I gave them permission to do as a whole raft of papers were thrust under my nose in a steady stream the next day, right before I had to leave to catch my plane. I asked the unit manager whether that arrangement would give them more money and free up their help."

"Well, yes, of course," the administrator had said a little crossly. It had been a long, hot meeting that to her mind did not accomplish anything for a most uncooperative patient, and she had other things to which she needed to attend. Did this difficult woman really think they did not take every federal dollar they could get? Their state budget was in shambles, and their nursing home was a large one run by a church organization with many Medicaid patients and not enough staff. She would ask the hospice nurse, who was there tending other charges, to stop in at her brother's room to explain the situation. In spite of the form that had been taken care of, he was still his own man, and he would have to sign for the service or turn the decision over to her.

When I agreed to have a hospice nurse come and explain the situation to my brother, one instantly appeared and the unit manager ushered us quickly from her office. Had a button been pushed that I hadn't seen?

But I liked the hospice lady, who sat with me in the hall and explained that no, there hadn't been a significant change in my brother's medical condition, but this simply meant my brother would get more attention in a nursing home setting where the staff was overworked and sometimes undertrained as well. "Are you a volunteer?" I had asked. All the hospice workers I had known in Portland were volunteers who did this work out of compassion and usually at great sacrifice of their own time.

There had been hospice workers for Eloise, too, but I didn't know whether they were volunteers.

"No," the woman smiled. "I'm not a volunteer. This is a fairly well-paying job. Don't worry about me."

So we went into his room together, a double occupancy room with a sheet divider, and I woke up my brother, who had been quite incoherent that morning. I did not expect him to agree to this arrangement. The nursing home staff had said he had refused hospice before and was belligerent and unpleasant about it and had even accused them of trying to kill him. He might object to even the suggestion, I said somewhat apologetically to the hospice worker.

Now this was the most amazing thing, I later wrote my nephews. Once he woke up, my brother was positively charming and excessively polite to the hospice nurse. Yes, he would agree to go on hospice, he said, but he did not expect to die soon. Three of his four grandparents had lived to be over ninety, he informed the hospice worker, so he would be likely to live that long, too, so he would get his money's worth out of them. Thank you, he said as the hospice woman gathered her briefcase to leave. My sister will take care of the paperwork. It was so kind of you to come.

I was glad to get home to my husband and the Nude Beach. "It was terrible," I told Jim, "terrible. The next morning when I had to sign all the papers, I went to see him again before I left. I made sure that Tami's name was on his chart as a family contact, and from now on I'll send letters to her—she's promised to read them to him." He was no longer the congenial patient of the afternoon before. His legs were drawn up almost to his chin. When I told him my plane was leaving soon, he didn't want me to go. They didn't feed him, he said; they were trying to kill him. His bed needed to be changed, but when I got the aide, he resisted because he didn't want them to screw up the TV so he couldn't see the sports programs that he watched incessantly.

Finally the bed was changed, and everything was clean again. "It is neverending," I said to Jim, "and I'm not sure I ever should have gotten involved at all."

When I went to the Nude Beach the next morning, I ran with the dogs in the wind. Gulls screamed above the water, and for the hour I was there I forgot about my brother and thought only of the river. But when I got back into the car I leaned my head on the steering wheel for a long time.

I didn't know what to say to him anymore that last morning, and we were both crying. There was a dead cockroach on the floor by the window in a strange Kafka-esque parody of Bobbie's position. I lay down on the bed beside him and smoothed his hair. He dozed, and I wanted desperately to leave, but finally I dozed. As small children we had slept in the west room together, and the night our mother died, even though I was twenty-one, I left my bed in the south room and curled up beside him until we both finally went to sleep.

⟂

The tundra swans left first. For weeks they had been flying in practice formations across the river from Ridgefield Wildlife Refuge to the island. I almost always saw them when I went to the Nude Beach, in the morning and in the afternoon. They called to each other in low whistling hoots, and after the dogs had run, I drove to the end of the island road and opened the windows to enjoy the musical clatter that floated across the field from Cunningham Lake. Swans, Canada geese, snow geese, the thin higher notes of pintails, the rubber-ducky sound of widgeon; it was a great festival of waterfowl staging to migrate. Each morning I lingered a long time, separating their voices. Surely this was what once had kept Lewis and Clark awake all night in their camp across the river. In an often-quoted section from the journals, they complained about the cacophony of bird sounds. Served them right if they couldn't sleep, I thought uncharitably. Their explorations paved the way for the great migration westward that wiped out the Native American population. And they were always eating dogs, even when there was plenty of wild game.

"Better look out, Pani," I said aloud. "You're getting a little pudgy. You better start running more with Devi instead of snooping along in the tide line. Just across the Columbia at the large village on Lake River, Lewis and Clark bought twelve dogs from the Quathlapotles, and they ate them all." Flocks of cranes landed close to the road, and my own pampered canines, unmoved by the incessant avian conversation or the appetite of the Corps of Discovery, finished licking their wet paws and fell asleep in the back of the car. "You're pretty lucky pups," I said to their disinterested forms.

Then the snow geese left, too. Once hunting season was done they had begun to feed in the outer pastures, and when the clouds broke in the morning I stopped behind the snowberry hedgerows, trying to catch the moment the sun would turn their wheeling forms golden as they rose in small flocks to feed elsewhere for the day. But suddenly not a snow goose was to be seen—only the long-legged cranes who leapt and danced in anticipation of their own journey. Spring was truly here, and soon purple martins would be back on their gourds on the houseboat deck just beyond my upstairs study window.

Orlando, I had scrawled in the sand that morning. I had written it in my notebook, tried all sorts of free association scribbles, but it wasn't until twelve pelicans sat on the shallow pond in front of the Nude Beach parking lot that I remembered the postmark on the card in the carnival glass bowl. *A funny old bird is a pelican ... Wish you were here. Bob and Kate.* Had my brother remembered that or was it just by chance that he landed in Orlando? Perhaps, it occurred to me suddenly, he rather than our mother had taken the postcard from the carnival glass bowl.

How did you end up in Orlando, Bobbie? He had looked at me blankly and had not answered.

It was not as if he didn't remember or didn't know what I was asking. It was more as if the answer was encased in a glass cube with no opening, as if he could stare at it himself but could not share the compartmentalized contents in any way.

I imagined a stack of these cubes in his brain; memories in boxes that he dared not pry open, three-dimensional loss. My own brain reeled with pain for him when I thought of this. I should have known I wasn't going to get off easy, that simply finding him would not exonerate me of nearly thirty years of neglect, and that the required follow-up would be more than a letter dashed off every month.

I was not, however, prepared for the barrage of phone calls from Tami. Two things were apparent in these calls: that Tami was genuinely concerned about my brother's health and that Tami had waited a long time for some assistance in his dismal situation. This made me feel sad and uncomfortable. When we abdicate our family responsibilities, I thought, they inevitably fall on someone else. Usually the calls were merely messages on my machine. Tami phoned after she got off work, and with Florida three hours ahead of Oregon, her calls usually coincided with the my afternoon hike with the dogs.

"I went to see Bob today and read him that letter you sent with the check. The sore on his hip is getting better now that the hospice lady comes and uses some special pad filled with air and some special salve. You don't need to send me no more money to take care of things. We come to see Bob 'cause we love him. Well,

Gary don't come much, but now and then my daughter comes. We bring him Milky Way candy bars and soda pop. It's lemon-lime he likes, but I think the nurses take most of it." The southern drawl of the message was so thick that I often had to play the message twice. I felt a twinge of shame, faced with the depth of Tami's honest and prolonged concern for my brother.

"And who is my neighbor ... a certain Samaritan, as he journeyed, came where he was: and when he saw him, he had compassion on him ... which now of these three, thinkest thou, was the neighbour unto him" (Luke 10:28-33)? Once I had known the whole passage. *Love thy neighbor as thyself. Love thy brother.* This was getting pretty heavy duty and bothered me at night.

For months now I had corresponded with my brother's older son, and I enjoyed his conversational contact with news about his children. My own sons were far away and busy with their own lives; my older son, with my only grandchildren, lived in France.

"I got a letter from Dad today," my nephew said in an e-mail. "Dad didn't write it, of course, the nurse did, but I was awfully glad to get it even though it was brief and didn't say much. I totally believe Dad loves me and always did. If things had been different with my parents (both had more than their share of issues) my life would have been different, too, maybe for better, maybe for worse. I have been fortunate to believe always that life is good. I look at my past and know that God was watching out for me and making sure I was provided for. I remember as a kid while living with my grandparents that Dad would spend a weekend with us. We would pore over the baseball scores and talk about who was leading the league in home runs. In college I started doing fantasy sports. I used to do baseball, basketball, and football. I only do basketball now, and I don't let it get in the way of other things I should be doing, like playing with my kids."

The very suggestion of fantasy, even my nephew's assurance of controlled fantasy, scared me, and I replied in a long e-mail.

"When your dad was a child in rural Iowa there was no fantasy football, of course, no computers and not even any TV in our house, but he spent hours at a primitive precursor of what you described—so many hours that it frightened my mother. He had a game called 'electric football' that consisted of merely a light bulb under some kind of plastic transparency on which one put a paper overlay of offensive and defensive plays. He constructed elaborate charts with players' names and statistics and lived as entirely in that world as kids today live in Internet games. He was a lonely and isolated child with no effective male role models at all, and our grandmother's farm was a sort of fantasy existence where we all lived in the past, surrounded by dead relatives, especially our grandfather's ghost. We shared a peculiar childhood from which it seems to me my brother never escaped. We had a game that seems especially troubling now where we constructed an alternative family with a strong father, who constantly brought us presents. I think you are a step up on the evolutionary scale in a family with more than its share of eccentrics to be so at peace with your father at such a young age. I was in my fifties and had to write a book to come to peace with mine.

"Your father's failure to participate now in any physical therapy that would strengthen his muscles and allow his legs to move from their painful contracted state baffles me, as does his total refusal to respond to any meaningful questions I try to direct his way. He has constructed a mental cocoon around all painful memories, and he only stares at me vaguely if I try to ask him anything of substance. I do know that, before I lost touch with him, he loved you boys fiercely, and it must have been and must still remain at some level of his consciousness the greatest sorrow of his life to have failed you so miserably.

"I admire you for this trip you are planning to take to Orlando in June so your family can meet your father, just as I admire your brother Bill for taking Nina to meet him some years ago. Do prepare your children for the fact that their grandfather is in extremely poor health. I advise you to go to the nursing home alone first. Tami tells me there is some kind of pump they are using on his hip to drain the sore. He seems to be excited that you are coming and tells her again and again about it. He has asked the nurse to buy presents for the children with his money.

"I cannot imagine quite how this visit will be for you. I'm glad you have your religion to help you through this. Yes, his life is miserable now, and yes, it is largely through his own doing, but you have a tolerance for his addiction that was a long time coming for me. I say unequivocally that it is easier to deal with difficult relatives when they are safely dead. You, however, have the remnants of a real person to deal with, and that will surely be a challenging ordeal.

"Now, in late spring, the Canada geese bring their new goslings to the houseboats to show them proudly, and the eight o'clock eagle takes its daily flight up the Channel. I wish you good fortune in your journey to Orlando, and I send you and your family much love. Aunt Barbara."

I was more confident of my nephew's affection now, and finally I was able to sign my e-mails with no hesitation. But I continued to worry about any suggestion of fantasy. I copied lines from earlier writing into my notebook.

When my brother and I were very young, we both slept between flannel sheets in the west room in the winter. Our mother would heat the water for the water bottles . . . the air outside the covers was like ice. Well into the night we would play the Game. It was a dialogue that involved a large imaginary family with a father. No one knew of the game but us, but our mother would come, finally, hearing our voices, and tell us to go to sleep.

We played the game for years. It was an ongoing dialogue. I do not remember that we ever talked of real happenings or people to each other. Certainly we did not talk of our real father . . .

In early adolescence I wanted out of the game, but my brother persisted for a long time. I can see him, standing at the foot of my bed in the south room, weaving a long monologue to which I refused, uncomfortably, to respond. I felt disloyal when he finally left the room (*The Violet Shyness of their Eyes*, 37).

◯

As I followed the dogs in their mad dash across the road, Big Indian arrived in his truck. Had he driven through the streets of Portland without a stitch of clothing? I had not seen him often, never in the morning, and we had not exchanged more than a casual wave. I noted now with a quick glance that he had slung a sort of cape over his shoulders before he crossed the road. That was a nice native touch. Island natives wore cedar capes and woven conical hats during the winter as protection from the cold rain. Sometimes the men wore skin ponchos.

Sneaking another hurried glance, I could see that what I had thought was a cape was a poncho, too, a Mexican-looking poncho for tourists, at that. A concession to the rules of the beach, I thought with some amusement, as there was no one around but me. When I reached the hard sand along the water, I turned upstream toward Social Security Beach, a deviation from my usual downstream direction, to compensate for the distance I lost because of the sturgeon carcass.

This big dead sturgeon was an inconvenience. It was close to the Blue House, not far from the End of the Nude Beach sign, but it shortened my customary route. The first day I saw it the dogs had not bothered it at all; they were, in fact, quite intimidated by its enormous size. It looked like a small whale on the sand. I measured it in boot length; it was over twelve steps from one end to the other, and the tail had been sliced cleanly off, maybe by a ship's propeller. It was a shame, I told the Lady-Who-Picked-Up-The-Trash when I saw her in the parking lot later that day, as that sturgeon was way above the legal limit for fishermen to keep, so it must have been quite an old fish. It wasn't stinking yet, but would she mention to someone at Fish and Wildlife that the carcass was there? Surely they keep track of such things, at least when the fish was of unusual size. It would be nice, of course, if someone stronger than I was could shove it back in the river. I'll mention it, the Lady-Who-Picked-Up-The-Trash said, but they'll just say let nature take its course, and she was right.

Two days later the flesh torn open by gulls and vultures had started to ripen. I managed to distract the dogs before they sidled against the putrid fish, but that was just luck and I knew it. Obviously it was time to change the route and turn around before the last stretch of beach. Maybe an unusually high tide would pull the large carcass back into the river or some of the night revelers would bury it.

Today the eastward upstream swing afforded an unusually colorful sunrise. I raised my arms above my head. "This is the day the Lord hath made: Rejoice and be glad in it." Funny how those Bible verses stuck with you all your life, I thought, even when you professed not to believe and had listened to the weatherman explain wind conditions and how the smoke from a fire on the mountain would probably create an exceptional sky this morning. With the application of just elementary science one knew exactly how this day was made and even the reason for the spectacular sunrise. I played with the verse in my head, but I was unsuccessful at rearranging it. "Well, Eloise, you win this one," I said aloud. "It screws up the cadence to take the Lord out."

I whistled for the dogs and turned downstream. I could see that Big Indian had brought out a kayak, but at the moment he seemed to be swimming. As I approached to pass him he rose from the water, a shining, wet form like a slender seal with flowing black hair in the bright sun. Well, not quite like a seal. More like Adonis with such an athletic build; of course, I didn't say that, I just said good morning and continued walking.

He called after me. "I've seen you before. I recognize your dogs."

I half-turned. "Most people do," I said. "The dogs seem to have recognized you, too, or they might have barked. You looked like a seal coming out of the water." He laughed, and I noted that he had picked up his poncho and placed it strategically in front of him.

"My name is U-wey-ii," he said. "It's Cherokee for River. My friends always forget how to pronounce it, so I tell them to call me River. I come here for my medicine in the morning."

"Medicine? Are you a shaman? I have a friend who's a shaman."

"No, I'm not a shaman. Actually, I've just gotten off work. I do white man's medicine, you know, putting together all those pills everyone takes, and then I come to the river to renew myself with natural medicine. What could be more healing than this?" He pointed at the sun; it had now split the clouds into a more general red haze that floated over the Washington valleys between the mountains.

Funny I hadn't seen him in the mornings, I thought, considering I came almost every day myself. Maybe I came too early, or it could be he went to the Nude Beach up the Columbia at Rooster Rock. White man's medicine—was he a doctor, a pharmacist? His language sounded professional or at least educated. I wasn't sure I wanted to be fostering the conversation, but he seemed nice enough, friendly, and with his poncho covering him, at least minimally dressed. I was always amused when young men hastily covered themselves or turned away modestly at my approach, as if their grandmother had appeared on the beach and found them without their clothes.

"You must not come here often in the morning," I said "I'm here almost every day to run the dogs, which I need to do now, as they are loping far ahead."

"Usually I come at sunset," he said. "Do you ever come then? I've seen you in the winter in the afternoon."

"No, I mostly come in the mornings. Even in the winter I come early in the afternoon. Have a good swim, River. U-wey-ii. I'll work on the Cherokee."

"I saw you disappear through the trees with the dogs, and I left you a present," he said. "It's under your windshield wiper."

I didn't look back or wave. This was strange, how he offered his name. I didn't know anyone's name on the Nude Beach, certainly none of the Odd Ones. Even the perfectly normal lady who picked up the trash for Fish and Wildlife with plastic gloves had no name in my mind. Just for a moment I felt slightly nervous, but he didn't follow, and when the beach curved I glanced back to see him fiddling with his kayak. Or was it a canoe? As I looked eastward into the sun he seemed like a ghost from the past leaning over his slender craft.

Well, that was a rather romantic idea. Now if I were a fiction writer, I thought, projecting a conversation with Madeline, or better yet, some sort of science fiction or fantasy writer, I could turn Big Indian from a tall, lanky Cherokee into a shorter royal Chinook with a faintly slanted forehead, an apparition or reincarnation from the lost world of the Wapato Island natives who had been so decimated in the Great Pestilence. Hopefully, he would not be out for revenge for the ravages of white man's diseases; no, surely not this nice young man. Or I could make him part of a parallel universe like the Black Ash Alley shadows, a visitor from another time zone who just happened to intersect my own sunrise. I should probably call him River, now, and dispel my worry about the name I had given him in my mind, Big Indian, but it was more honest to stick with my own shortcomings when writing nonfiction. He seemed so friendly, so open to conversation, unlike others I had encountered on the beach—the strange photographer in the Blue House or the Builder who could only talk about the wind. I did not feel in the least afraid of him, which was a good thing since he was still on the beach when I came back, this time with his poncho around him. In fact, he obviously meant to take up camp for the day in the tidy shelter he had fashioned with his kayak and some poles.

"You're wise to stake out your space," I said. "It's going to be such a nice day you'll have lots of company as the sun warms up." Had I actually been the one who initiated the conversation that time? I tried to remember later when I was telling Madeline.

"How old is this guy anyway?" Madeline asked.

"I don't know. I think he's fairly young—he certainly has coal black hair."

"You can't always tell," said Madeline, and she proceeded to relate a story about a writer she knew about who had married a Native American and everyone, including Madeline, thought the woman was robbing the cradle. "Turned out the guy was older than she was—considerably older, in fact. What did he leave on the windshield?"

"Just a feather," I said a little uncomfortably. My husband, when I told him about it, hadn't been amused at that, either.

"This guy is strange," he said. "Better stay away from him."

But he hadn't seemed strange at all that morning on the beach. He'd asked me whether I lived on the island and whether I knew anything about its past. He had not lived in Portland long, but he wanted to connect to the real history of the place. Learning all he could about the natives of new places had become sort of a religion with him because he realized so much of their history and culture had been lost. Would I share a story from what I had learned about the island? I was rather charmed by that, so I did. At first I remained standing, a bit awkwardly, with one foot on the log beside him, but finally I sat down, too, and told him a story.

Down the road from the moorage where we lived, a small sign identified where Fort William had existed for a brief time in the 1830s when an East Coast entrepreneur named Nathaniel Wyeth had grandiose ideas of challenging the Hudson's Bay Company's dominance in the fur trade. There was absolutely nothing left of this small trading post now but the marker and a few colorful stories, such as when two men got drunk on the formaldehyde that one was using to preserve specimens and got in a fight over a native woman, resulting in the first white man's murder on the island. I'd recently learned another story that involved a young native girl who died.

According to a popular history of the Wapato people, the naturalist named Townsend, who was working from Fort Vancouver, used Fort William as his base, and in his explorations and gathering of specimens he went to the very end of the island by Warrior Rock.

I asked the man named River if he had been there, and he shook his head.

There's a three-mile trail at the end of the road, I said, before you come to the lighthouse and Warrior Rock Beach, where Lieutenant Broughton almost met his Waterloo. In the late 1700s, Broughton was sent up the Columbia by George Vancouver's expedition to explore and map the region, and at the end of the island he was met by warriors in several canoes with carved bows and sterns. Lewis and Clark, only a few years later, described these canoes as the most beautiful they had ever seen. Fortunately, for Broughton that is, he had a guide who could communicate with the Chinook.

Big Indian was staring intently at his kayak. I would like to have known what he was thinking, but he remained silent so I returned to my story.

In his explorations at Warrior Rock, Townsend found a recently embalmed body of a young girl. She was laid out in ceremonial clothing in a burial canoe, and he was so taken with the perfect example of Chinook burial customs that he wanted to send the body intact back to the East Coast to be studied. He knew the mummy would have to be removed clandestinely, however, as there were recent offerings that indicated that someone, perhaps a relative, was tending the young woman's grave. So Townsend secretly moved the body to Fort William and secured it under the floorboards to await transport east on a commercial ship.

A few days later a young native lad came alone to the fort because he had found the empty burial canoe. You have taken my sister's body, and you must give it back to me, he said, presumably in the Chinook language. We have special ceremonies that must be observed, and I am honoring my sister by following our burial customs. I must have her body.

At first the men at the fort denied any knowledge of what the young man requested, but day after day he returned with the same sad entreaty. Finally, moved by the young man's obvious sincerity and sorrow, they relented. They removed the young girl's body from its hiding place under the floorboards and returned it to her brother. The last they saw him, he was heading down the path to the end of the island, weeping and carrying his sister's body on his back.

I stood up, feeling almost nervous; perhaps I had offended him with the story.

"What a good brother this young man was to care so much that his sister be properly buried," the man named River said. "I have many brothers and sisters, and we were taught to look out for each other, especially to keep each other safe."

I knew about that. I had been taught that, too. I turned away from him, and the dogs got up from the sand to follow.

"You could come back for the sunset," he said almost gently, "and share more stories over a glass of wine."

I shook my head and gathered the dogs on their leashes. He did not get up from the log or look at me directly. When I reached the car, I noticed the feather under the windshield wiper, and I put it in my notebook for a marker. I felt sad and a little confused, certainly ashamed of the naturalist in the story. I seemed to be feeling ashamed of myself as well, something no doubt to do with my brother, or had I left out details from the story that I should have included? What had I written about that Nathaniel Wyeth person, anyway? Before I started the car, I flipped through my notebook to find what I'd paraphrased from John Kirk Townsend's journal.

A New England entrepreneur named Nathaniel Wyeth established Fort William in 1834, along what is now Sauvie Island Road, an ill-starred trading post that lasted only two years. He observed the bones of the natives who had died in the Great Pestilence. He did not record any sympathetic feelings for even the infants who had died, locked in the dead mothers' arms. Instead he wrote to his wife that it was propitious that Providence had seen fit to eliminate the natives at such a convenient time. It was truly a blessing, he said, because it had saved him the troublesome task of eliminating them himself.

When I got back to the houseboat I copied two selections of special interest concerning the Wapato Island natives from Townsend's journal:

The Indians of the Columbia were once a numerous and powerful people; the shore of the river, for scores of miles was lined with their villages . . . Now, alas! where is he?—gone;—gathered to his fathers . . . his place knows him no more. The spot where once stood the thickly peopled village, the smoke curling and wreathing above the closely packed lodges, the lively children playing in the front, and their indolent parents lounging on their mats, is now only indicated by a heap of undistinguishable ruins. The depopulation here has been truly fearful. A gentleman told me that only four years ago, as he wandered near what had formerly been a thickly peopled village, he counted no less than sixteen dead, men and women, lying unburied and festering in the sun in front of their habitations (*Narrative of a Journey,* 170).

Of even more interest was the exact incident I had described in somewhat imperfect detail to the tall Cherokee that day.

February 3d, 1836.—During a visit to Fort William, last week, I saw, as I wandered through the forest, about three miles from the house, a canoe, deposited, as is usual, in the branches of a tree, some fourteen feet from the ground. Knowing that it contained the body of an Indian, I ascended to it for the purpose of abstracting the skull; but upon examination, what was my surprise to find a perfect, embalmed body of a young female, in a state of preservation equal to any which I had seen from the catacombs of Thebes. I determined to obtain possession of it, but as this was not the proper time to carry it away, I returned to the fort, and said nothing of the discovery which I had made.

That night, at the witching hour of twelve, I furnished myself with a rope, and launched a small canoe, which I paddled up against the current to a point opposite the mummy tree. Here I ran my canoe ashore, and removing my shoes and stockings, proceeded to the tree, which was about a hundred yards from the river. I ascended, and making the rope fast around the body, lowered it gently to the ground; then arranging the fabric which had been displaced, as neatly as the darkness allowed, I descended, and taking the body upon my shoulders, bore it to my canoe, and pushed off into the stream. On arriving at the fort, I deposited my prize in the store house, and sewed around it a large Indian mat, to give it the appearance of a bale of guns. Being on a visit to the fort, with Indians whom I had engaged to paddle my canoe, I thought it unsafe to take the mummy on board when I returned to Vancouver the next day, but left directions with Mr. Walker to stow it away under the hatches of a little schooner, which was running twice a week between the two forts.

On the arrival of this vessel, several days after, I received, instead of the body, a note from Mr. Walker, stating than an Indian had called at the fort, and demanded the corpse. He was the brother of the deceased, and had been in the habit of visiting the tomb of his sister every year. He had now come for that purpose, from his residence near the *tum-water,* (cascades) and his keen eye had detected the intrusion of a stranger on the spot hallowed to him by many successive pilgrimages. The canoe of his sister was tenantless, and he knew the spoiler to have been a white man, by the tracks upon the beach, which did not incline inward like those of an Indian.

The case was so clearly made out, that Mr. W. could not deny the fact of the body being in the house, and it was accordingly delivered to him, with a present of several blankets, to prevent the circumstance from operating upon his mind to the prejudice of the white people. The poor Indian took the body of his sister upon his shoulders, and as he walked away, grief got the better of his stoicism, and the sound of his weeping was heard long after he had entered the forest (*Narrative of a Journey,* 174-6).

⌒

I drove back to the moorage with all the windows open. I felt like crying, would have cried if it would have alleviated my concern for the dogs' eyes or my frustration over the whole situation, but as it was, crying was unlikely to do either. My eyes watered anyway. The dogs knew they were in trouble, bad trouble, and sat in uncustomary positions on their haunches all the way home. Pani, the more sensitive to disapproval, nervously glanced from side to side, and Devi, whose eyes were the primary object of concern, lifted one paw tentatively every minute or so as if to rub at them, but each time she had to quickly put her paw down to retain her balance.

Why had I stopped at Social Security Beach? I never did that, ever, though I had considered it other mornings when pressed for time, because I didn't want to disturb early fisherman. That morning there had been no fisherman cars, thank god, I thought now, as all those garrulous old gaffs probably would have enjoyed the show. "You are a slave to those animals," my husband often complained, "a self-appointed one I might add, and there is no harm whatsoever if they miss an occasional run. When you're pressed for time just let me take them around the lake in the park." Good advice, for sure; why hadn't I done that?

For one thing, Jim was on the Deschutes River in central Oregon for a few days, fishing. Thank god, I thought again, because that gave me some time to clean up this mess. Yes, he was right, I was a slave to the dogs and their early morning pleading eyes, but I was a slave to the Nude Beach as well, to the gray-blue sky, to the burst of freedom I felt with the dogs when I first emerged from the cottonwoods onto the open stretch of sand. Figuratively my mind threw off its clothes.

Which was another reason, I thought angrily, that I never should have stopped at Social Security Beach. No psychological sense of freedom there, no nudes, not even in the figurative sense. Just way too many old careless fishermen who left their half-empty bait containers behind them, and families who came with their kids in the afternoon and left candy wrappers and spilled potato chips, a perfect draw for any kind of garbage-scavenging varmint. "Just a short spin," I promised the dogs as we drove across the island and parked in the uncustomary lot, "and you won't have to get your free-run exercise by chasing each other around my living room in the houseboat. Go find an osprey to fixate on and follow, Devi. And Pani, stay out of the garbage."

Before I even got the car locked the dogs had crossed the road on a frantic tear, gone over the dike, and Devi's wild yips had begun. Good, I said to myself, as I climbed the wooden stairs that made this beach so attractive for the old men, there must be gulls flying or maybe Devi has already sighted a cruising osprey, which would give her plenty of exercise on this short run. Then the yips stopped. Why was it so quiet?

As I topped the long grass that covered the dike, I saw that it was not a large bird that the dogs had found, which was tantalizing Devi with lazy circles; it was a skunk, a young one that looked no bigger than a black and white cat, and its backside was turned toward the dogs. A crazy, chaotic circus ensued. Seeing that both dogs were unwisely crouched in attack position, their heads lowered, noses pointed forward, I began to screech, a totally worthless exercise. They ignored me entirely, and I ran as fast as I could down the dike in hopes of diverting them out of range of the spray.

The skunk, obviously a young one, stood its ground and fired. Pani got the spray in the left ear, but Devi got it full in the face. Pani backed up out of range. I grabbed at her collar, lacing my fingers around it, but the dog was squirming too violently for me to attach the leash. Devi dove down into the sand, rubbing her face with her paws and rolling over and over, literally tearing at her eyes. Had the dog been blinded? Just that week I'd read an article about the damaging potential of skunk spray; how it could possibly, in sufficient quantities, permanently blind an attacker. Devi, I screamed, again to no avail.

Oddly, the overwhelming smell wasn't quite like skunk but a sort of wild, almost crushed-evergreen-gone-slightly-moldy odor. Maybe the skunk was too young to really smell like skunk. With a terrified Pani bouncing behind me, I tried to grab Devi, who kept writhing in the sand and digging at her face. Fear momentarily overwhelmed my anger. My god, was she really blind?

Apparently not. The crazed dog staggered forward and leapt again toward the skunk. Dragging the unwilling Pani with me, I lurched, trying to intercept her. This meant that all three of us were back in firing range. For the next two weeks, every time I closed my eyes I saw that lifted plume, the pink wrinkled iris with its distended black pupil aimed right at all of us. I grabbed Devi's tail and pulled but it was already too late. The skunk loosed another volley that hit Devi broadside before the dogs and I did a backward summersault down the slope in an awkward, by now truly skunk-smelling embrace. This time, flat on my back, I had both dogs by the collars, but the entire world, after our crazy spin, was completely distorted. I could physically feel the smell seeping into my pores.

As I held the dogs against me so Devi would not resume her foolish attack, the unruffled skunk began its leisurely inverted march over the dike, lifting its feet daintily in the tall grass. Slowly the world righted itself, but somewhere in the sand I had lost the dog leashes. This is your own fault, your own fault, your own fault, my head throbbed. People who keep their dogs properly on their leashes do not tangle with skunks.

I was a good ten miles from the moorage, so I had no choice but to put the dogs in the car; besides, I smelled as bad as they did. A terrified Pani was still trying to pull away, and Devi was rubbing her eyes in the sand. After my dizziness had subsided and Pani calmed, I coaxed the dogs up the dike. Then I went back and retrieved the leashes. Topping the dike again, I saw the skunk, a small form in the distance sauntering saucily across the field. Pani watched out the window while Devi lay down and closed her eyes. The car reeked.

All this led to a canceled doctor's appointment, a totally wasted day of scrubbing dogs, and a one-hundred-and-twenty-dollar bill for skunk baths at the pet store when a pungent odor remained after my Internet remedy of hydrogen peroxide and baking soda. The pet store wash didn't solve the problem either and turned Devi's back a mild yellow. I called a dog-owning neighbor who swore by a feminine hygiene product to cancel the smell. I tried that, even on my own hair, and it became a race against time to make the houseboat habitable by the time my husband returned from the Deschutes.

That night Jim scrambled up the rim-rock that lined the canyon of the Deschutes and called from his cell phone to check on our well-being. I immediately confessed the skunk encounter to prepare him for the fact that the smell issue had been somewhat imperfectly resolved. He was mostly worried about Devi's eyes, but once I assured him the dog was now seeing just fine, the implications of the scenario I described did not entirely escape him. It was possible, he warned me, depending on the severity of the situation by the time he returned, that he might suggest the dogs and I spend a few nights in my study. His marriage vows did not include sleeping with skunks.

By the next morning, however, it was back to the Nude Beach. A light mist somewhat reactivated the smell on the dogs. The wide expanse of sand that stretched along the river harbored no long grass or foliage that would likely conceal skunks, although I waited until I had perused the shoreline before I let them run. Why was I here again, really, I asked myself. Why didn't I just give it a rest for a day and take the safer walk around the lake in Wapato Park? Was I, too, an addictive personality, unable to inhibit my own self-destructive behavior? If so, I thought, I was surely not in the same league as my father and brother. I was not in a deeply introspective mood that morning; I was just glad I no longer smelled like a skunk.

We truly were incorrigible, all three of us, I thought, two long-haired white dogs and their white-haired owner. I could not quite explain, even to Jim, what this early morning Nude Beach foray with the free-running dogs meant to me, but the meditative experience it provided had become a necessity for my writing. Even fully clothed, I felt the freedom of unshackled social constraints that allowed my mind to expand. The dogs focused on swallows that swooped over the water for the morning hatch. Devi no longer pawed at her eyes or indicated any loss of vision. Both dogs had forgiven me for the multiple baths of yesterday, and I had forgiven them for their intrusion into the life of a skunk as well.

When I turned back, the mist had stopped and the eastern clouds were stippled a lovely gray-mauve color like goose-back feathers. It occurred to me as I walked how very fond of these crazy pups I was now, in spite of all their foibles. I no longer confused their names with the old dogs. Not that I had forgotten the other dogs, but I had plenty of room in my heart for dog souls, other animal souls, both wild and domestic. I sang this crazy song each morning as we drove across the island, Pani barking and Devi doing her strange human-like warble in anticipation of our unfettered run. I sang it now, but the dogs were too far ahead to hear and too happy enjoying their own unleashed time on the Nude Beach to bother with me. Devi yipped at a gull she was trying to herd, and Pani barked wildly at absolutely nothing as she dug furiously in the sand. It was a good thing, I thought, that not even Jim could hear this.

      ○

Big Indian was back. I hadn't seen him for a few weeks, and for the most part, I had not thought of him. On Friday morning, however, mist that had floated over the Coast Range during the night got between the island and the sun, forming a double rainbow with refracted light. It arced over the fields on the island side of the road just as the sun rays crested the clouds over the river. Wasn't a double rainbow a native sign of something-or-other? Perhaps Big Indian would know, but he wasn't there to ask. River, I practiced. U-wey-ii.

So Saturday was a surprise. When I arrived with the dogs, the entire beach was empty, just the way I liked it. Usually on warm weekends there were as many as ten boats anchored off shore, but that morning, when I expected a whole flotilla, not a single boat was to be seen. Good. It was always a hassle to keep the dogs from barking as I passed. Maybe there had been some sort of skirmish. The Man-with-the-Metal-Detector had told me there were definite turf wars out there by late summer. The tide was full out, the sand hard for fast walking. There was no wind, and the whole flat river tilted in a golden sheet. Pani dug furiously at a Frisbee half-buried in the sand, and Devi ran in circles, herding the wheeling gulls. I could see clear down to the lighthouse on Warrior Rock, and blue mist layered between the Washington hills on the other side of the river.

The walk went too fast; reluctantly I turned around at the End of the Nude Beach sign. I had managed to get past the site of the big sturgeon carcass without the dogs even showing interest, or worse yet, going over for a roll. That might have ruined a morning of otherwise spectacular beauty, requiring another pet-store skunk wash. The sturgeon was temporarily ensconced in what must have been several layers of sand, and the huge mound was covered with white beaver-skinned poles and branches. With typical Nude Beach humor someone had placed a wooden sign on it with big spray-painted letters. DEAD, it said.

I was over halfway back to the entrance for normal-people-who-just-like-to-take-off-their-clothes when I saw him. At first he was just a silhouette against the glare of the water, but sure enough, as I got closer, the cardboard cutout turned into Big Indian in all his unclothed glory, knee-deep in the water and bowing toward the sun. This tall Cherokee-River-U-wey-ii, whatever I should call him, was strictly in the Noble Savage tradition; that neo-classical body right out of Benjamin West's *The Death of General Wolfe*, I thought.

He saw me and waved. I waved back, but I veered off toward one of the informal entrances through the trees because as Jim had said, this was getting a bit strange, and I wanted to get back home, anyway. But he came striding my way ,and the dogs turned around, anxious to greet him, so I turned around, too. "Don't go yet," he called. "I want another of your island stories. I find your energy so refreshing." So I waited. I certainly wasn't afraid of this fine-looking specimen of humanity just because he wasn't wearing clothes. But, I admitted later to Madeline, it was more than a little disconcerting to talk about island art under the circumstances. "I may be old, Madeline," I said, "but I'm not dead."

The story I told that morning was of a native image from the island that was in the Portland Art Museum. "You'd like it," I said, "considering your penchant for this particular condition. It's the image of a nude, a sort of crude sculpture on a big slab and the most human features are the ribs and the genitalia. The face isn't very realistic at all. It's on the third floor of the museum," I continued, suddenly feeling awkward telling him about this particular artwork, as if his nudity made any difference to me or I even noticed it, for god's sake. I should have described the Spedis owl in the little case instead, except I didn't know the story behind it, and I wasn't absolutely sure it came from the island. "I know a man—he's dead now—who knows the man, a tug-boat hand, who dug it out of the mud during low water time in the Multnomah Channel. I found out about it because a woman who lived on the moorage, until her kids carted her off because they suspected she had Alzheimer's, was once married to him."

"The tug-boat hand?"

I conceded later to Madeline that I was a little flustered during my presentation of this story. I tried to concentrate on his shell necklace instead of looking down.

"No, not the tug-boat hand, the guy who knew him and bought the image from him. He later sold it to the Portland Art Museum when he screwed up his life and needed money. When he was married to my friend who used to live at the moorage, they had the stone slab in the entryway of their house and because of his abbreviated anatomy, they called him Big Dick."

"Big Dick?" At that River threw his long black hair back and roared with laughter.

I turned the conversation to him and I learned all sorts of things. He was a surgical RN, he said, and repeated how he worked thirteen-hour shifts three days in a row. "When I leave I tell my fellow-workers that I'm going for my own medicine on the beach, and they understand. I work with good people."

I understood, too. I came here for a sort of medicine myself.

He was from South Carolina and all the rest of his family was still there. He was the fourth of nine children. His uncle had seventeen kids. Lots of Cherokees came back, you know, after the Trail of Tears, he assured me. Between the brothers their family stretched all the way south to Florida.

I would forgo thinking about Florida and my brother this morning. "Your father and uncle are certainly doing their part to repopulate the tribe."

He laughed, but he added a bit wistfully that it was rather lonely without any of his family. "Wait," he said suddenly. He stood back and made a frame with his hands like a student in art class as if he were considering a photograph or a painting of my face. "Do you know what a beautiful picture that makes with the sun behind your white hair?"

"Well, thanks," I said, "but this beach has enough crazy photographers." I told him about the Naked-Red-Girl in the snow. He looked concerned. By that time we were almost to the road, and he ducked modestly behind a bush whenever a pickup with a boat roared by on the way to the Gilbert River ramp. Word was that the fall chinook were running.

"I like your good energy and your stories," he said. "Really, that would have made a good book cover shot with the big disk of the sun around your hair."

I was the one to laugh now. "The cover for a book entitled *The Wisdom of Old Women*. How old are you, anyway?"

"Older than you probably think," he said a little sheepishly.

"You'd better get busy and find a cute little wife and hold up the family traditions," I told him. "Start your own little Cherokee tribe out West."

"That's not so easy," he answered wistfully.

Maybe you'd have better luck if you put on clothes; your physical perfection is a bit intimidating to the normal female mind, I thought later.

"You'll find someone; maybe not a Cherokee." I told him another story, abbreviating it because the dogs were almost pulling me across the road to the car. "I knew a Native American storyteller once. He used to come to my classes when I was a teacher, and he told me that nothing was easier than getting a white woman in bed. It's a great time to be Indian, he told me. These gals, especially the middle-aged ones, they would die to get in bed with an Indian."

"Really? Not this white woman, obviously," he grinned. "Are you married? I so love talking to you."

"Yes, I am, U-wey-ii," I said, trying to pronounce his Cherokee name that meant river the way he had pronounced for me on our first meeting. His disappointment was so apparent that I would have touched his shoulder were he not too far away.

"I have a husband who is quite a guy, a husband to die for. He wouldn't care if we just traded stories." I smiled, and he smiled and waved as I crossed the road.

"He's a lucky guy, your husband is," U-wey-ii called, and after I got in the car I noticed he had placed another feather under the windshield wiper.

"Now, Madeline," I said later at the John Street Café, "this young man surely did just want to trade stories." I sighed. "But whoever would have thought at my advanced age that I'd get a story like this?"

Madeline regarded me with amusement. "It occurs to me to wonder how you might have responded to him *if* you had been single—age difference aside, if it even exists. Would you have let yourself be drawn into a sexual relationship? I would have found the whole thing flattering—and a little bit frightening. But I might have gone for it."

I had to think about that.

"No . . . yes . . . No, I don't know . . . I don't think so, though. Not because of any scruples, but because I am somewhat body-shy and careful at this stage of the game. And I'm glad to be past that aching, longing, surge-through-the-thighs-I-don't-care-what-this-costs-me-I-want-it-and-I-want-it-now feeling. Getting old is a relief."

❧

When I left the John Street Café, I didn't go directly home even after I crossed the bridge to the island. It was a hot day, too hot for early September, and Jim was fishing in Montana, not available for our afternoon hike in the coolness of Forest Park. The Nude Beach would be crowded with naked flesh on a Saturday that was more like summer than autumn, the cars stacked three deep in the parking strip, so I didn't want to go there. I pictured the dogs belly-up, legs splayed, asleep on the cool tile of the kitchen floor in the houseboat. The second walk of the day would have to wait until the sun disappeared behind the West Hills Ridge. Oak Island, I decided, would have to do at the moment. At least I could do a short hike to Sturgeon Lake mostly among trees.

Oak Island was not a separate island in spite of the name. This slightly elevated ground, with its unusual rock and gravel, was a remnant of an older island that survived submersions during the

Pleistocene floods. Dust billowed behind my car on the long gravel lane that ended at a yellow gate. Huge oaks, some of them so old they were purported to have been standing well before Columbus, clustered over a grassy savanna. I walked slowly through the trees that shaded the first part of the path with only the whine of autumn insects breaking the silent heat. A brief emergence from the oaks as I turned toward the lake was a painful experience in blond and honeyed light; what a relief when the shade resumed.

When I reached the corner where the path turned to follow the lakeshore, I sat down on a solitary bench with a view of the water and Mount St. Helens in the hazy distance. A plaque on a short pillar commemorated a young man: "Keith Boells Lobdell who loved Sauvies Island. Oct 4, 1957 – July 18, 1986," it read. He had not quite twenty-nine years of life. I had been told once that his death was a suicide, but I wasn't sure of that. Wasn't twenty-nine my very age when I had tried to emulate my father? Had I succeeded, I would have been already dead for nearly forty years.

The bench was still warm from its exposure to the sun, and I moved back into deeper shade and sat down on the grass. A short time ago in an e-mail exchange with my religiously inclined nephew, he had respectively asked in genuine interest, "Just what do you believe, Aunt Barbara?" I had replied with my usual evasiveness. I like the idea that the Bible implies there is no real name for God, I had written in answer. That means to me that all religions are to be equally respected. But I always thought about his e-mails later and searched for Biblical support for my position. Exodus 4:14. I AM THAT I AM, God said (in capital letters in the King James version) when Moses asked what name he should give the Israelites for the deity who had sent him.

Even as a child the phrase had been a mystery to me, one more applicable to humans than to God. What a strange grammatical declaration, although the Revised Standard Version had changed "that" to "who." I am that I am, I repeated softly, returning to the less anthropomorphic construction. Was it sacrilegious to use that phrase in describing oneself? I must remember to put that in the notebook.

Returning from the Nude Beach one morning a few days after my e-mail discussion with my nephew, I had turned on the radio to hear a segment about Lucretius and his long poem, *Of the Nature of Things.* Just as the writing in which I was currently involved had been initiated by the radio interview with the neuroscientist, so this interview led me to days of research and readings of the Roman poet and his Greek predecessor and inspiration, Epicurus.

Not since graduate school had I spent so much time on the Epicureans and their amazingly modern philosophy. Atoms and the void, the enjoyment of this life for that would be all there was in the present form, the ultimate recombination of everything—body, spirit, soul—into other natural forms. No wonder I had all these unfinished manuscripts in my drawer; I spent too much time just enjoying the incredible beauty around me. Too much dog-walking, too much idle research in anything that caught my attention, too much mountain climbing, Eloise had admonished me, disappointed that I had not finished a work I had started about the Sutherlands who had come from northern Scotland to start the Scotch Grove Presbyterian Church.

My lonesomeness for Eloise was almost palpable; a selfish lonesomeness, I admonished myself, for the discussions with Eloise were the vehicle by which I resolved the ongoing tension between my early religious training and my adult secularism. Lucretius was certainly hard on all religion, both Greek and Roman and especially mystery religions that emphasized a life after death. They provoked an entirely unreasonable fear of the natural process of death, he argued, by presenting a version of an afterlife that defied any physical possibility and was based on punishment and rewards. Could I have discussed this latest publication on Lucretius with Eloise, who had not been afraid of death and had expected some kind of reunion with relatives?

Probably not; Eloise's belief in a traditional Christian after-life had solidified as she embraced her own death, and she had become less willing to engage in philosophical speculations.

Long blanched strands of flattened grass neatly swirled like combed hair under the oaks and, suddenly overcome with sleep, I lay back, my arm across my eyes, my white bone almost visible through my glowing skin. What would it have been like to have already been dead forty years? Would I have simply separated into the infinitely rotating supply of atoms, as Lucretius had said, my present self, body, mind, soul, expanding to recombine with other atoms, becoming an infinitesimal part of a bird, an insect, or a distant star?

Perhaps it was the heat, or it could have been the indistinct call of sandhill cranes that came from the other side of the lake, the first cranes I'd heard this autumn, that provoked my lazy response. There was such a thing, I decided, of taking all this religion business and maybe life and death too seriously.

Life itself is enough, I thought. Later I wrote that in my notebook below the line I transcribed from Exodus.

"I am that I am."

The nuthatch began its nasal twang, quail rustled in the bushes, and occasionally I heard the skate of ducks landing on the water.

This had become an unexpected rehearsal.

I slowed my breath, relaxed my eyelids. Through the smell of mud along the lake and dusty weeds that lined the path came the waft of distant death picked clean by circling gulls.

Chapter Three

For two days we owned a horse, a lovely four-year-old mustang mare, a *grulla*, which was the color Madeline had always wanted, ever since she read her first two-gun western novels as a teenager.

"The hero's horse was a *grulla*," Madeline said. "And he loved that horse so much that it made an indelible impression on me about the way one can relate to animals as well as the way one can use language to convey deep emotion. The death of the horse literally tore this man apart. 'He walked the *blurred world* to the horse' when he realized it was dead. I've never forgotten that phrase and the raw emotion it conveyed."

My own landscape blurred just listening to Madeline. The bay horse of my childhood had been struck by lightning, and each time a loved animal died, it was the same. *Blurred world.* I was almost embarrassed at the depth of my grief.

We were not at the John Street Café during this conversation; we were driving to the Wild Horse Corrals near Burns to attend the Bureau of Land Management's Kiger Mustang Auction. If you buy mustangs, warned Jim, who was beginning to worry that this fantasy was getting out of hand, just keep driving south.

Six hours from Portland to Burns.

First, we talked about horses.

We had no intention of buying a horse at this auction. Or two horses, for that matter. We had lately decided that one horse would be unfair, both to the horse and us. We harbored quite separate dreams about horses. And as for the horses, well, horses were herd animals and needed company, so we should each get a horse and keep them together on some island farm, not two yearlings that had elementary training, but older horses.

It was the Keiger mustang studs that brought the most money at the Wild Horse Corrals, the ones with the lateral stripe down their backs and the zebra stripes on their legs. The Youth Challenge girls got the yearlings of more ordinary colors, ones that hadn't been sold at the horse corral auction. We would buy our horses, maybe even next year, we told each other, as soon as our books were sold. I would be happy with a bay but Madeline still hoped for a *grulla*.

"I didn't know for a long time that it was a color," said Madeline. "Gray-blue in different shades, darker face mask and the same stripes and markings as the Kigers. It's because of the dun gene. I never even saw the term *grulla* again for thirty years or so once I left the teenage western phase until I read Cormac McCarthy's *All the Pretty Horses*." Reading that, Madeline was swept up in nostalgia for the books of her childhood. She was glad to encounter the term *grulla* again. "We should see some *grullas* at the corrals," she said, "but I don't know if they make it to the Youth Challenge."

"We'll find a *grulla*, Madeline. We own this fantasy and we can make it turn out any way we want it."

Next, we talked about husbands.

"I'm trying to understand this," said Madeline. "You're going back to Nepal because of Jim?"

"*Only* because of Jim. I love Nepal, but I've spent way too much money going back and forth. But his company gave him the ticket for a retirement present, and he wants me to come along."

"I thought you had given up mountain climbing. Isn't it about time that Jim gave it up, too?"

I tried to explain.

I *had* given up mountain climbing—certainly twenty-one-thousand-foot peaks like the Imja Tze, which Jim wanted to climb. The last two times I'd tried really high mountains, I'd gotten sick. Last summer Jim and I were hiking on Mount Hood, only half the altitude of the mountain Jim wanted to try again in Nepal. I was standing in an incredible field of lupine, paintbrush, and cats ear above Timberline Lodge, watching climbers at the chute that went up through the Pearly Gates to the summit.

I'll never go up that chute again, I realized suddenly. *I'm too old.* I'd seriously hurt myself if I even tried. I'd never officially admitted that even to myself, and to do so made tears come to my eyes.

"It's not something anyone can tell you: you have to reach that point by yourself. Jim's not there, yet, but he'll get there, too, and it will be worse for him than it has been for me."

"So let him go to Nepal with his climbing buddies."

"His climbing buddies are too old, too fat, too infirm, or already dead, their obituaries in my Dead Friends file—that's what happens at this stage of the game."

The climbing rules in Nepal had been tightened so Jim had to sign up with an organized group to get a guide. That was most of the problem. Jim disliked groups where he didn't know anybody and he wanted me to come, at least for the trek. Our younger son had come up with the money to join us at the last minute; if I'd known that was going to happen, I might have been able to refuse. Now I'd already paid for the nonrefundable ticket.

Madeline looked at me warily. She knew how I felt about leaving now. "What about this thing with your brother?"

"I'm just going to hope he doesn't die while I'm gone. I'm only going to do the first part of the trek and come home early."

I wasn't going to bore Madeline with all this again. Bobbie had been taken off hospice—something the nurse said almost never happened—because he had gained too much weight for the new Medicare guidelines. It was inconvenient that I was the one responsible for my brother's medical decisions, but I could hardly expect his kids to drop everything in their busy young lives to take responsibility for him when he neglected most of his fatherly responsibilities for them.

This most recent trip to Florida had been the worst of what seemed like so many trips I had lost count. I had delayed e-mailing his sons for a week after I returned. "I'm sorry not to have written sooner," I began my letter. "I couldn't decide whether to gloss over my depression or whether to be totally honest, but I guess I'll go for honesty. Even though they have taken him off hospice because he gained too much weight, I think he is worse mentally, Bob, than when you were there in June. He now refers to himself in the plural *we* no matter what he says. 'We saw the squirrel by the window this morning.' 'We don't like it when the nurse changes the channel.' I asked him if he knew who I was, and he looked at me as if I were the one with mental problems. 'Of course, you're Barbara,' he said. He refused this time to try to go for a ride in the car. Then he asked me to rearrange the bulletin board pictures of your children and to dust off Bill's graduation picture and put it where he could see it.

"His head is full of sports statistics. He told me that in the 1960s, Iowa had played Oregon in the Rose Bowl and Iowa won. He knew the score, who scored what touchdown, who made the winning play. Maybe he has so many football scores in his head that his brain doesn't work anymore. The nurse asked me if he'd ever been diagnosed as obsessive-compulsive.

"When I mentioned that he looked better because of all of the hospice care, he repeated that he expected to live to be ninety. I took that remark as an opportunity to ask him, just in case I was still around and in charge of making any medical decisions in twenty years, what were his feelings on end-of-life care—did he want life support machines? Yes, he said, by all means. If they don't work, and you're dead, what then? I asked. Do you want me to ship your bones back to Scotch Grove? Mom bought cemetery lots there when we were just little kids. Absolutely not, he said. It's way too cold in Iowa."

"I'm just going to hope my brother hangs on," I repeated to Madeline. "It's a worry, a monumental one, but I need to do this for Jim. Sometimes there are things you do just because you love the guy and he's your husband."

Madeline knew all about loving husbands. She had been married for over thirty years, and after her husband died, she did not write for a long time. When she finally wrote about her own grief, she did it in third person, as a character in a novel. We talked about that: fiction or nonfiction for conveying personal pain, how to convey the wrenching truth of grief without evoking pity.

"I got a letter from a woman," said Madeline, "who told me that her sister had lost her husband to cancer. She told her sister that every time she tried to express her compassion she choked up because she simply couldn't imagine what it had felt like to go through that long, sad ordeal with a spouse. Her sister sent her my novel and said, you must read this book. It felt exactly like this."

This whole death thing was like a scab at this age, something to be worried, to be picked at. So we talked about death.

"Madeline, do you ever feel there is anything left, really?"

"No. The only quasi-spiritual thing that happened when my husband died was that the dog started barking, howling, in fact, and ran around and around the house."

"You never felt his presence in the house again? People always talk about that."

"No. I think in some way, before my husband died, I didn't *believe* in death. I was so shocked by the nothingness of it that it sucked the meaning right out of life, if that makes sense. It took me years to work through that."

Blurred world indeed, I thought, only this was no two-gun western, this was Madeline's life, and I should shift this painful conversation. I was spared because we had reached the corrals and could go back to talking about horses.

That *believe* thing again, I thought a few days later when reviewing the conversation with Madeline while I was walking on the Nude Beach. People who believe in life after death . . . What Eloise believed, which was a conventional Christian heaven; what my friend Jan believed, which was some sort of further evolution of our spirituality; what many in Nepal believed, that a son was required to usher his father into heaven; and what Madeline, with her practical mind, believed—a nothingness. Why this continual nagging about what I believed myself? The clouds that arced over the river were gray, blue-gray even, like the mare in the raffle at the Kiger Horse Auction. *Grulla.* I'd bought two raffle tickets at ten dollars each.

"What are you doing?" Madeline had remonstrated.

"Pretending," I said. "That's the most beautiful horse I have ever seen: the slight dapples, the silver sheen of the coat like snow-clouds with sun behind them, dark ear tips, mysterious colors blending into each other."

"What if you actually win?"

"We can share her and next year bid on a yearling from the Youth Challenge."

"We don't have any place ready to keep a horse."

"I already have that figured out. Your friend with the Lipizzaners will help us until we find a place."

Madeline looked at me and shook her head, but she was intrigued by even the chance for such a beautiful horse. "I'm not paying my ten dollars for the second ticket unless we win," Madeline said firmly.

Grulla, I had scrawled in the sand. The dogs were far ahead so the word would stay until a container ship passed or the tide returned. Then I was thinking about writing: How could this be? I asked myself. Madeline was so much more orderly and methodical in her approach to writing, to money, to life, so much more practical than I was. Yet Madeline could write fiction, even science fiction, construct complicated alternative worlds. How odd, that I, the impulsive one, an indulger of impossible fantasies, could only write nonfiction. If it hadn't really happened, I simply couldn't finish the piece. Even in transcribing well-documented events, I agonized over telling the truth. Given the way our minds operated, shouldn't it be the other way around?

And this life-after-death business. Madeline—with her parallel universes, her short stories with unexplained people who appeared from nowhere or strange tears in the sky from which long-dead people descended on ladders, her validation of her friend's half-woman ghost—should have been the one who was still haunted by the possibilities of a post-physical-death existence. Yet, I was the one, not Madeline, who always left the issue unresolved, repeatedly indulging in conflicting ruminations.

Of course, we hadn't won the mare; I'd never won anything in my life except a hammer at a farm store drawing when I was a child. Nonetheless, we'd spent two glorious days wandering through the horse corrals, picking out this colt or that, setting the price we could not go beyond in the auction, having perfectly serious conversations about horses and pretending the mare was already ours.

Grulla, I thought, even searching in the clouds for a darker line that would form the lateral stripe in the shapes I rearranged in my mind to a blue-gray mare with a mane lifted in the wind. I whistled for the dogs and composed my own dictionary definition of the term. *Grulla*: a mysterious blend of dark and light; a northwest Nude Beach color of indefinite sky and mist.

◎

The grand piano in the vast lobby of the hospital seemed to be playing itself. The song was an old Presbyterian hymn, but it didn't sound like any kind of recording because it had no orchestration swelling between verses or after the chorus. It sounded like someone had just sat down at the piano and played a song from memory for a distraction from more painful thoughts. I thought of going over to see whether the keys were moving, but I was on the other side of the spacious room. Was it a player piano? How odd in this formal, modern lobby. The only player piano I'd ever seen in action, an old battered upright, had belonged to my Sunday school teacher Ella Clark. I shook my head gently to avoid jarring my sinuses, congested from the overnight, sleepless flight, before I crossed the lobby to the desk. "Room 3721," the receptionist said.

I stopped at the restrooms across the hall from the elevator to splash cold water on my face. I could feel it coming. My Nepal trip was going to be doomed from the beginning, and it was mostly, I thought resentfully, because of my brother. I felt deeply ashamed of myself and again held the cold water against my face. My brother was suffering, not just the usual miserable condition of his daily life, but the excruciating pain of continual coughing with pneumonia wracking his thin frame.

Jim and I had been away overnight for a hard, fast practice hike on the mountain in preparation for trekking in Nepal, and when we got home the light on the phone message machine blinked accusingly. Tami had called. The nursing home had called. And then a doctor with an unpronounceable name left a message as well. It was a garbled message, and I could only make out the last part, which was almost a shout: "Somebody has to make a decision here," the accented voice said. "I can't just ram a tube down this man's throat. Somebody has to take responsibility here, and your number is first on the list."

First I called Tami.

"I went to see him at the nursing home, and he wasn't there," Tami cried hysterically. "Where's Bob, where have you taken him? I screamed at the nurse, but she said they didn't have to tell me nothin', that I wasn't Robert's family, and I said you just look on the chart, his sister put my name on the chart as family, so she did, and then they told me he was at the hospital so I went there. You gotta come," Tami wailed. "I'm telling you, you just gotta come. They ain't doin' nothin' to help him at all, and he coughs and coughs. He fell out of bed six feet to the floor in the nursing home, and they didn't find him for an hour, maybe longer than that. He's gonna die, and then what do I do?"

So I went. A week later, I thought, and I would have been in Nepal for a month, out of reach of all this.

I called my nephews, got a ticket on the red-eye, and arrived in Orlando at six o'clock in the morning. Try to come home by Wednesday, Jim said, or you'll never be able to make the Nepal flight. The money for the trek, the money for the ticket, the half I'd already paid for the house-sitter—all down the drain if I didn't go. That gave me less than two days to deal with this. How could I be thinking of money at a time like this?

But *this* was a pretty big one. It did not look at all as if Bobbie would be able to hang on until I returned from Nepal. Because my brother had been removed from hospice, the "do not resuscitate" order had been rendered invalid, which meant the nursing home had the legal obligation to send him to the hospital when he fell out of bed and subsequently developed pneumonia.

It was unclear to me that I had ever signed such an order, such a flurry of paperwork had been shoved under my nose, I said to Jim when I got off the phone with Tami. Why didn't someone, the nurse or the social worker or the hospice employee, explain that when you sign this particular form you are giving the medical community permission to wash their hands of all care that would keep him alive? Had my brother known that signing up for hospice entailed a "do not resuscitate" order? How could I be sure of that when I wasn't even cognizant of it myself? They said he had fought the service before when he was "his own man." I remembered full well that he had explicitly told me he wanted them to use whatever means were available to prolong his life.

"Wait," I said to the exasperated doctor in the hallway outside my brother's room, who would not even give me enough time to sit down and explain. "It is not that I wouldn't make that choice for myself; I certainly would. I'm just not sure I have the right to make the choice for him when he has expressed contrary wishes. Right now he is still his own man. Could we try to ask him?"

"Are you out of your mind?"

Why was this doctor so angry, so impatient, so *mean*?

The vet with the old dogs had been so kind. Each time I had held the dog in my arms when he administered the needle.

The doctor wheeled to face me squarely.

"What is the big deal here, anyway? You signed the form once when he went on hospice before. Your brother can't swallow, so we would have to cram a feeding tube down his throat and into his stomach. Can you imagine how that would feel in his curled-up position? There is no way it could be done without a considerable amount of pain. I'd never do this to a relative of mine. *Never*."

"Couldn't we ask him for a verbal consent?"

"Look," the doctor said firmly. "This man does not have the mental capacity to make that kind of decision now."

Did that mean they'd already asked him and he'd said no?

"I'm sorry," said the doctor. "I have to go right now. I'm going to be out of the hospital for the weekend, and you won't be able to reach me. You need to make the decision now."

The blurred world.

"Okay, I'll sign," I said. "I don't want him in even more pain. I'll sign."

"Good. I'll have them call the hospice nurse, and they'll get the papers ready again. They'll remove him from the hospital, take him to their facility—it's a nice facility, a comfortable place to die. This won't take more than a few days now. Without the feeding tube, he won't last long."

The doctor wheeled and started down the hallway. Then he stopped and came back to me. I stood beyond the doorway where my brother lay, but I could hear the rasp of his breath. Had he heard any of this? I wondered.

"I'm sorry," the man in the white coat said, taking my limp hand and at last speaking slowly. The anger had drained out of his voice, and I felt an odd sympathy for him. How many times a day did he have to deal with something like this?

"I really am sorry, but there is absolutely nothing you can do to help him now. You have made the right choice."

After standing in the hallway a moment, I went in to try to talk to my brother. He seemed to be sleeping, so I simply stood beside him, as there was no chair for a visitor. He looked already dead to me, a skull without many teeth. He was hooked up to some kind of machines that grunted softly in a low rhythm. Would he be able to talk at all if he woke up? "Bobbie," I said softly, and he opened his eyes. He coughed mightily, and the gurgle sounded like thick water bubbling, the last sludge in a big rusty barrel before it slid down the drain.

Hello, he mouthed. He tried to clear his throat in a horrible spasm of coughing and finally managed a whisper.

I had to lean close to hear.

"You look good," he whispered. "It's nice to see you."

I moved as if to sit down on the bed.

"Don't sit there," he whispered. "You don't know how much our legs hurt. You must leave now, or they won't feed us."

They wouldn't feed him anyway; they couldn't because he didn't pass the swallow test. There were rules to follow.

"They're trying to kill us here." He twisted slightly in the bed, and I could see his scabbed back where the hospital gown hung open. Was this from his fall out of bed when no one found him for an hour? One welt with a scab was bleeding slightly, and a plump red drop fell to the white sheet. Cherries in the snow. I did not remember why that phrase was lodged in my brain until I was back on the Nude Beach reliving the scene. Yes, Uncle Howard, that was it. *He took a stick; gave him a whack.* Our father and the song about the goat.

"I'll go in a minute," I said. "I just came to see you before I went to Nepal for a month. I'll come again as soon as I get back."

Why didn't I tell him about the order I was to sign?

He stared at me with his head falling to one side. Does he know who I am? I wondered, but then he said something about our childhood, about the fun we had together when we rode the horse. "Do you remember that?" he croaked.

"Of course," I said, but when he tried to speak again, even the whisper was gone. His eyes closed with exertion.

"I'll be gone for a month," I told him, stroking his hair, "but I'll call your sons before I go. I'll tell them you love them." He nodded his head. "Do you want me to say anything else?"

Tell them I'm dead, he mouthed. Then he either passed out or went to sleep, and when I couldn't rouse him, I sat in the hallway with my back against the wall. I sagged with weariness. This, I thought, is definitely nonfiction. If this part of my life were fiction, I would surely leave out Nepal, which seems so incongruous, but in reality it is the Nepal trip with my husband that is forcing me into the painful crisis of taking charge of my brother's death. Otherwise I could try to wait this out, insist they take care of him or *something.* Or feed him, so if he died at least he wouldn't die thinking I wouldn't give him food. I couldn't think straight.

That's how it is in real life, all sorts of inconvenient insertions into the storyline, even when an important tragedy threatens to consume you. I found myself thinking of when my mother died. It was close to the end of the term in graduate school, and I missed a final exam in linguistics. I didn't even visit the professor for three weeks afterward, and when I did he just stared at me thoughtfully. Did he believe me? Did he hear this excuse often?

Should I be crying instead of still in a state of numbed disbelief at her death? We all have to learn to cope with our parents' dying, he said, when he gave me an extra week to study. But I never even took the exam, because I still couldn't think about linguistics.

The hospice social worker came down the hall and extended her arm to help me get up from the floor. Somehow we landed in a little alcove, conveniently tucked away from the hall traffic. After I finished the crying business, while the hospice social worker sat there with discreet calm doing her paperwork, I called Tami, miraculously connecting with her on the first try. "I need to know, Tami, whether he ever said anything to you about what to do with his body when he died."

"Just once," said Tami. She was so relieved that someone was there to help her that she started crying again even though she was at work. "I could lose my job for taking a personal call," she said. "We talked about it once when I was reading the Bible to him, which I did sometimes. I said I didn't want to be cremated; I wanted to be there in one piece for the resurrection. Bob laughed when I said that. Not too much chance for any resurrection for me, he said. My body can just go to science."

But of course he hadn't taken care of that, I thought almost angrily. When you don't take care of your life, you don't take care of your death, either. Well, at least that gave me something to work with; I knew he didn't want his body sent to Iowa. Wasn't there a research hospital in Orlando?

The hospice lady hesitated. She would make the calls, she explained. "This has to be handled through a regular funeral director, you know. It's not like you can just take them in a taxi." She had handled a science donation just last week, so she would call the same gentleman for a quote.

How nice this lady was. If the doctor had talked with her calm voice, I could have managed to get my thoughts straight. I leaned back in relief, conscious of how much my sinuses were throbbing.

"The total cost would be $5,095," the hospice lady said, handing me a piece of paper on which she had written the information.

"*What?*"

To *donate* your body to science? We were literally blocks from a university hospital. So the hospice lady repeated in detail for me what the funeral director had said.

Anatomical donation: $3,000. Embalming: $995. Funeral director: $495. Service utility fee: $185.

"If I could spend $5,000 to make his life better, I'd do it in a minute," I told the hospice lady apologetically. "I have to think about this. What do they do when no one claims the remains?" What if I had never found him at all?

"There's always Potter's Field," the woman told me. "The state takes care of it. It happens all the time with the homeless. We can call the state for you when he goes."

Potter's Field—that had something to do with the Bible, the pieces of silver for Judas, a burial place for strangers. No, not Potter's Field. Our mother had bought cemetery lots for us as children.

I thought of the story I had told Big Indian, of the lad with the bones of his sister on his back.

"I'll figure this out and call you from Portland in the morning," I told my husband.

"Do what you have to, Barbara; Eloise left the money," said Jim when I called from the airport.

"It's not about the money; it just seems there must be a more sensible way to get this taken care of."

And in the end there was, a research clearinghouse called Medcure, with headquarters in Portland, but miraculously, with an office in Orlando. They handled body donation with no cost, and I managed, with what seemed like a thousand phone calls, to get all the arrangements made before I went to Nepal.

"And what are your wishes for the final disposal of the remains," the woman at Medcure asked delicately. After the research organizations have finished, the incomplete remains were cremated and either sent back to the family or disposed of at sea; in the case of Orlando it would be the Gulf.

I managed another call to the nephews. Buried at sea, they decided, his ashes scattered in the Gulf. Thank you, Aunt Barbara, for taking care of this for us.

The poor Indian took the body of his sister upon his shoulders, and as he walked away, grief got the better of his stoicism, and the sound of his weeping was heard long after he had entered the forest.

All that happened the next day in Portland, but I had one remaining hurdle before I left Orlando. Once again, I faced a raft of papers, this time cognizant that I had indeed signed the order that my brother was not to be kept alive with heroic measures— or any measures at all.

We were taught to look out for each other, to keep each other safe, U-wey-ii had said.

I had betrayed my brother's wishes, however merciful the act seemed to me.

"It won't be long," the hospice social worker said, echoing the doctor's words. "He failed the swallow test, and they don't last long without intervention. I'll call his sons when he goes."

Surely, I was at least obliged to tell him what I had done. I stood in the doorway and watched his troubled sleep, but in the end, I could not make myself go into his room and try to wake him.

In the lobby the old Presbyterian hymns filtered through a group who had gathered, talking quietly as if someone had just died. The piano sounded almost childish, like someone practicing with only one hand, the way I used to do when it was my turn to play hymns for Sunday school. Curious that such an odd tape would be playing. I walked across what seemed acres of floor tile to check on the grand piano in front of the window. Its keys were not moving like those on my Sunday school teacher's player piano had moved, when as a child it had seemed to me that an invisible ghost must be sitting on the bench.

☙

We were talking about writing, but we were not at John Street; we were talking on the phone. I had come home from Nepal too sick to go anywhere but for short walks with the dogs on the Nude Beach. They could run free, and I could stop and sit down on logs, not even caring how wet the soaked wood made my jeans.

"You have an advantage in fiction, Madeline," I complained. "When the plot gets too cluttered you can strike whole sections out. Even in nonfiction, had I stuck with Men in the Family, the Nepal trip might have been important—a central metaphor, in fact. I could have developed Jim as a really positive addition to my life, a man who took me up mountains, so that the decision I made to accompany him to Nepal was a logical one, considering what he had given me throughout our relationship. I could have used the mountain climbing to show how my son—with a different name than Robert, with a good, solid step-father who taught him to climb real mountains instead of engaging in impossible flights into fancy—had escaped the genetic curse."

Of course, I reminded myself later on the Nude Beach, I had decided early on that this men in the family issue wasn't genetic, and I couldn't make it so unless I massaged the truth. That led to this notebook entry:

> Is there truth in memoir, or is the form almost by definition fiction? That which is finally written down has been filtered through one's memory, a most self-serving mechanism.

"So who made the summit of the mountain?" Madeline asked.

"Not Jim. He made it over the high passes, but he came down with a respiratory illness—along with the rest of the group, I might add. You might say they passed the banner to youth. Our son and a young Norwegian woman were the only ones well enough to leave base camp and summit. One man had to be carried down in a pressurized bag even before the group reached base camp. At least Jim made it down under his own power."

"And you were already home?"

"Yes. What was an adventure in my forties was an ordeal in my sixties. The romance of trekking in Nepal hardly entered my mind this trip. For one thing, it was jarring to see the porters on cell phones stepping around yak dung. And I thought about my brother the whole time."

"And then he didn't even die while you were gone."

"That's right."

Surely I did not sound irritated.

"Unbelievable," sympathized Madeline.

I had been right that the episode with Bobbie just before we left for Nepal had cursed our whole trip. Not only was I emotionally drained from the forced, hurried decisions I had made, I was physically exhausted, fighting a sinus infection, before we even left Portland. And after that it got worse, much worse.

I returned home to another bureaucratic tangle with my brother, who, in spite of all the predictions, had not died during my absence. Strangely, and against all odds, everyone I talked with assured me, he had rallied once he was in the clean and quiet hospice facility; in fact, even without the feeding tube, the pneumonia had subsided after three days while he was virtually comatose. Once again, his resilience exceeded expectations. So much so that he had to be transferred back to a nursing home instead of remaining at the hospice facility. Yes, he was still under hospice care, but there were rules to follow, guidelines with penalties, and hospice needed the room for someone more convincingly threatened with imminent death. This time there was no bed for my brother in the familiar place, so he was transferred to another nursing home altogether.

"We never thought to put a bed-hold on for him, and no deposit had been made to keep the room," the administrator at the original nursing home apologized. "When they take them over to the hospice facility itself, they never bring them back."

I had a flurry of phones calls with a near-hysterical Tami. "They ain't takin' care of him there, and that sore on his hip has started up again. And he wants to go back to his old room, Barbara. You have to make them do that. It's his home, the only home he's had for years, since he left our trailer. There he can at least watch the squirrels out the window."

I was still too sick to fly to Orlando, but with daily phone calls and threats to notify superiors, I finally got my brother back in the room that he identified as home. The wound nurse was thoroughly scandalized. "I had that sore on his hip all cleared up," she reported emphatically. "I can't think what they did at that place to let it get this bad again, and it's only been a couple of weeks. I should report this to the authorities." But she probably didn't; Robert had returned from the dead, as the nurse had put it, and they were all equally baffled.

Then I got a call from the hospice nurse, who informed me that my brother would never last until morning, because there would be no intervention for the pneumonia this time—the proper papers had been signed—and he was in a semi-coma, quite incoherent. He would not be moved to the hospital, and it was unlikely I could get there before he died. When the phone rang again, I did not even check the caller ID, partly because my mind was numb and partly because I assumed it was the nurse again, calling to tell me he was already dead.

"Hello, Barbara, this is Bobby."

Bobbie? Oh, *Bobby*. Roberta, the half-sister.

"I'm so glad I finally caught at you at home," Roberta said cheerfully. "It's been months since I've talked with you, and I just wanted to see how you and our brother were doing."

Our brother? I had no time to summon any defenses and simply repeated everything the hospice nurse had told me.

"I'm sorry, Roberta, I can't talk now because I have to call my brother's sons. The hospice nurse said he is unlikely to live until morning."

"I'm so sorry, I'm so sorry," Roberta said with tears in her voice. "I'll call the sisters and let them know."

I'm sorry, Roberta, I'm really sorry, but I can't think of half-sisters now, I thought after she hung up. I've been less than a half-sister to my full-blood brother all these years, and I have that to deal with right now.

In all honesty, I didn't think of that line about being a half-sister until later, when I walked on the Nude Beach again, trying to make sense of what had happened in the few weeks since I returned from Nepal.

That was why this stretch of sand, thoroughly unpeopled even in the afternoon when the weather was as cold as it was in December, was so important to me. I needed the happy, innocent gamboling of the dogs, the vista of sky and clouds, sometimes, like that day when there was absolutely no wind, reflected in precise detail in the river.

◑

What was it that our mother had said?

You must never, ever blame them. Was that what I was still doing to these women who were so persistent in their attempts to reach out to me in kindness and love? Blaming them? How un-*Christian* of me to feel annoyed toward women who had been left by our mutual father in an orphanage, and how unhappy my mother and Ella Clark would be of my uncharitable attitude.

But I couldn't help it.

⟐

Madeline had called me, not even written an e-mail first, and her voice had been strange and surprised. "You have to come to John Street," Madeline said. "I have news; some things have fallen together since Monday, and it's too big to handle over the phone."

Had Madeline finished her book? Had she been offered an astronomical sum for an advance that would cover the cost of her horse? But when I finally got to the café, and we were settled at our customary table, the conversation was not about horses, it was about brothers.

"You know, Barbara, I said when you found your brother that I had a strange feeling that I would then find mine as well. Well, he's been found."

On Monday Madeline had received a letter from the Board of Pensions of the Presbyterian Church. According to this letter, her brother was a participant in a Retirement Savings Plan prior to his death. "Fidelity's records indicate that you are a named beneficiary on this account," she quoted from the letter in her hand. "To request a distribution of funds, please call . . ."

She was astonished, first of all, that her brother had worked somewhere long enough to earn a pension, and she wondered why he had named her as his beneficiary. Why not their mother, who was still alive in 2002 when he started the account? And how had he died? How long ago? Where had he been living? And how had the Board of Pensions gotten her address?

"Wait. So he's definitely dead, Madeline? Your brother is dead?" I had been so involved in my own brother's drama that I had almost forgotten that Madeline was missing one, too.

"Yes, he's dead. He died January 8, 2008." Madeline was trying to present this in a factual, unemotional way. She was not quite successful, and she was talking way too fast.

"Wait until we get our order taken." The pony-tailed proprietor smiled at his faithful customers and took our orders. "Okay, go on, but don't talk so fast."

It turned out that the Presbyterian Church had a policy of searching for beneficiaries when funds were unclaimed, and a woman in the Retirement Savings Plan office had diligently tracked Madeline down—this is what she learned when she called the number she had been given. She spoke to the very woman who had written the letter.

"I told her about the missing thirty years, and that I wasn't very interested in the pension fund, but in learning all I could about my brother's life and death. For some reason, telling her this, I was almost in tears."

Only the Shadow knows, I thought.

"The woman told me that my brother had died January 8, 2008, and that he had worked for a Presbyterian Church in Cincinnati, and she gave me a phone number for the church. Then she said, "Please let me know what you find out. It's such an interesting story." Later she wrote me in an e-mail, "Please know that God truly loves you."

"Unbelievable, Madeline," I said. "What was he doing with the Presbyterians when you were raised Catholic?"

This isn't fair, I thought. I have first claim on the Presbyterians if they are going to crowd into the action. Fiction or nonfiction, you need some sort of foreshadowing, Madeline, and you've never even mentioned the Presbyterians. But of course I didn't say that. "How was he functioning at all when you said he was not only an alcoholic but so disadvantaged with the family genetic abnormality—the mild retardation, the speech impediment?"

"I almost didn't believe it, either." Madeline called the church in Cincinnati and eventually hooked up with a man who had been her brother's supervisor when he worked there. For more than eight years he'd been a night custodian for the church. He'd been homeless before that, or so his supervisor had heard, but that was before his time. "'He was very quiet, a shy guy, but well liked,' the man told me." Madeline paused as if she were almost overwhelmed by this information.

You can have *my* Presbyterians for foreshadowing, Madeline, I thought charitably. The people of the Scotch Grove Presbyterian Church had been awfully nice to my brother and me. "Sounds like a happy time in his life; almost as if he had a family there."

"It does, rather. I wish I had known this at that time, had been able to see him there, or at least that my mother had known about it," Madeline continued, more as if she were talking to herself than to me. "I asked if my brother was drinking, and the supervisor hesitated but then said he didn't know. While he worked for the church, my brother had a small apartment and a car and liked to go fishing. Well, my dad had been a fisherman and had taken both of us fishing when we were young. I hadn't stuck with it. It was astonishing to hear that my brother had."

"A boy needs a father," our mother had said, but I didn't interrupt Madeline with anything like that; my family story certainly was not the tragedy of the day. Maybe this disappeared brother thing we shared was the kind of coincidence that could only happen in nonfiction, I thought fleetingly. In fiction it would seem too contrived.

In 2007, Madeline's brother had been fishing on a lake when he fell on rocks and broke his kneecap. While he was being treated for that injury, they discovered that he had tuberculosis. So he was off work several months, quarantined and in treatment for the TB as well the broken knee. When he returned to work that fall, the supervisor said he seemed to have lost interest in life. He was cured of the TB, but he didn't seem to care enough to rehabilitate the knee and was unable to perform his work. Within a few months, they felt compelled to let him go.

Madeline and I stared at each other. *One of those bodies of homeless men they find behind dumpsters.* But it wasn't quite that bad.

A year later, the supervisor received a phone call from a Salvation Army Officer in Albany, New York. The officer told him that Madeline's brother had died suddenly of a heart attack while working at the shelter. He was homeless then, but he was sweeping floors in exchange for housing and meals. They had found, in his paperwork, that he had once worked for a Presbyterian Church in Cincinnati, and they were calling to see if anyone at the church knew of relatives to contact. No one did, so he was buried by the State of New York and a Salvation Officer conducted a short service.

Neither of us spoke for a minute, and the waitress came to ask us if we were done eating, in spite of our almost full plates. We told her we were just engrossed in conversation, so she smiled and poured more water.

"Hooray for the Presbyterians, Madeline. I'm green with envy that you know all these specifics of his life."

"I find this so very strange and sad," said Madeline wistfully.

It occurred to me that it would have made a neat little turn in what I was trying to write about Bobbie if he had ended up working for the Presbyterians, considering his childhood and the Scotch Grove Presbyterian Church. In fiction that would make a nice tight circle, but that wasn't the kind of convenient detail that one could just add in nonfiction. And wasn't it odd, how important siblings turned out to be in this death business. But that would have to be considered later.

Madeline continued in a subdued tone, almost as if she were surprised at how sad she felt about all this. "I wish he could have gone on working for the Presbyterians and that he had died with people who were fond of him. I don't like to think of him becoming homeless again and dying among strangers."

"At least my brother had Tami there," I said, "and she was crying."

That wasn't quite true, I thought later when I was driving home, what I said to Madeline about Tami being there in the room with my brother when he died. That began to nag at me. This just proves it, I thought almost angrily. Nonfiction memoirs are not the way to get at the truth. They are, by their very nature, sure to be fiction because all events are filtered through the self-serving and consequently unreliable medium of one's memory. Wasn't this an absolutely perfect example? I had not intentionally lied, but already I had rearranged facts in my memory to alleviate my own sadness over my brother's lonely death. The hospice nurse had assured me that I would never get to Florida before he died, so I didn't even try. There's nothing you can do now and you have everything in order, she said soothingly. It'll be a miracle if he even lasts until morning.

If he doesn't die until morning, I thought, he will die on December 12, the anniversary of our mother's death.

After I talked to the nurse and called my nephews, I tried Tami's cell phone, and Tami was there in his room.

"Is he conscious at all, Tami?"

"Not really."

"Tell him I love him, Tami," I had said. "Whether you think he can hear you or not."

"It's your sister, Bob, and she wants me to say that she loves you."

I could hear him cough in the background, an awful wracking sound. It seemed he had said something. "What did he say, Tami?"

"Water, he said water, because he's so thirsty. Why won't they let me give him water?" Tami wailed.

"I don't know, Tami." Was it because I had signed the order? "Do it anyway."

But they had taken away the glass.

"Tell him again that I love him, Tami."

"Why wouldn't they let him have water? He's dying anyway, for Christ's sake," I said to Jim when I hung up the phone.

About nine o'clock the next morning, even before the hospice nurse got to the phone, Tami called to tell me that Bobbie was dead. "I should have come right away when I woke up, but I kept putting it off," Tami said. She was sobbing so hard she could barely speak. She had arrived just minutes too late.

It took me two rounds of Tami's tearful narrative to get the information straight. "So he has already died, then?" I had to repeat the question twice.

"Oh, Barbara, it was so awful. His eyes kept popping open when the hospice nurse tried to close them."

Well, he must be dead then. Why didn't I feel anything at all? Yes, this was December 12, all right, I had checked the calendar. The same day my mother had died. Why was everything about my brother always so confusing? I just wanted to get the information straight before I called his sons. I took the dogs to the river before I did that. Even at the Nude Beach I didn't cry. There would be plenty of time later, if I would cry at all.

We'll have that memorial service you wanted at the Scotch Grove Presbyterian Church when the weather has turned, I told my nephews. Late May or early June when your kids are out of school, and I'll get to meet all your families. I'll make the arrangements and cover the cost. By then the remainder of his ashes will have been scattered by the research people in the Gulf. Buried at sea, I'll put with his name on our mother's stone.

"I don't know what I feel," one nephew said. "Just emptiness, I guess. That makes me feel rather guilty."

"It's all a blank," said the other. It's hard to miss what you never had, I thought.

Thank you, thank you, Aunt Barbara, for taking care of this.

"Tami," I had said, "if there's anything among his belongings that you want to remember him by, please take it with you now before they pack up his things. I have told them that I want anything that is left behind sent to his sons, but you can take

THE NUDE BEACH NOTEBOOK   171

anything you want. You're the one who has been his family all these years."

"I took that little wind-up chicken," said Tami, who was still crying when she called me again later, "that little toy chicken that was in a fruit basket that Marge sent one Easter, I think it was. Sometimes when I came to see him he would say, make the chicken dance, Tami, and I would."

The wind off the river was cold and sharp as I walked behind the galloping dogs, and my face felt clean and good.

☙

Finally, after rescheduling the event twice, Madeline and I had connected with Anne's lesson on Patriot. Madeline had been friends with Patriot and Anne for a long time. I, however, had only ridden past the farm on my bicycle, staring wistfully at the Lipizzaner horses. The neatly fenced rectangular paddocks, the tidy barn, the house discreetly hidden behind fruit trees; it all radiated a certain classiness, I decided with awe, something far afield from my own informal experience with either farms or horses.

I was fascinated by the horses' names. Galaela and her three-year-old filly, Galamora. The naming protocol for a Lipizzan female was to begin the name with the same letter of the filly's dam and to always end the name with an *a*. The beach mist had pushed over the coast range that night, and the white lawn chairs in which Madeline and I sat to watch the lesson had been wiped down with a towel. Patriot worked through the warm-up routine and several exercises. As the lesson neared its end the trainer put on music, a Strauss waltz and then, as if on cue, the mist stopped and the still mostly obscured sun cast a weak moving shadow of horse and rider.

Until that day I had never heard the term the trainer called softly. Mine had been a farm experience with horses. I leaned forward to hear the trainer say the word again as Patriot trotted around the ring.

"Madeline, what is she saying?"

"*Piaffe*. A slow cadenced trot, almost in place," Madeline said, speaking in soft clipped sentences because she was concentrating on the horse. "Highly advanced dressage. It's a natural gait, but not all horses and riders can get the communication right." There was a slight edge to Madeline's tone at having to explain everything to this rank amateur when we should be watching in silence. Then it happened.

Patriot shifted into the soft, lilting, dance-like gait, and we all knew it: the horse, Anne, Madeline, and I, the rank amateur, who had never had a lesson in my life. I had only galloped my horse wildly through forest and field, but my throat swelled and I had to compress my lips sharply to stifle a sob. After a short time doing this dance, Anne and Patriot stopped right in front of us, and before Anne dismounted, she leaned forward and threw her arms around the horse's neck. Madeline took a tissue from her jacket pocket and blew her nose.

"Maybe I'll start lessons again," said Madeline as we were leaving. "Not to learn how to ride, of course, I know how to ride, but to take it to another level. I never quite understood myself until I took lessons last year how important they were; well, you saw today when we watched Anne on Patriot. It's all about communication between the rider and the horse. You have to get it just right so the horse knows what you're asking." Madeline suggested that we go to a couple of training clinics so I could see how this was done; she had gone to a ranch and worked horses with a trainer before she wrote about horses in her last book.

When I left the Lipizzaners that morning I went to the horse websites and looked for examples of *piaffe*. Later, I e-mailed Madeline.

"I've been thinking of *piaffe*, Madeline, and how it's related to writing, that communication of which you spoke. It has to do with the writer, the unwieldy body of language, the potential reader. When we came back Saturday from watching Anne and Patriot, I puzzled over exactly what it had been that made our eyes swell with that smooth switch that Patriot made. Anne, too, kept wiping her nose after she came back across the ring, and before she dismounted, she threw her arms around Patriot's neck. The horse looked so pleased with himself that I expected him to grin.

"I've just been watching clip after clip of *piaffe*. This may be, as you say, a natural gait for a horse, but the only time I've seen horses do it naturally is when they are checking out something strange and skittering around it or playing with another horse. I thought of what you tried to explain about the communication that works between horse and rider. And I thought about Anne's dogged dedication and her work on Patriot's education for the thrill of this transformation from the ordinary working gait of a trot to that smooth artful dance.

"You probably don't expect a Pulitzer with your next book, and I am certainly not in this thankless business from any expectation of money or glory. But we persist: leaning toward that transformation of language, the magic of a more pedestrian trot becoming *piaffe*."

My ruminations continued later at the Nude Beach. Madeline was a careful craftsperson, each word chosen slowly and methodically with the end result exactly right. I imagined her writing as if she were on a horse, a Lipizzaner like Patriot, turning her phrases artfully to a Strauss waltz, searching for the precise word that would convey the impression she intended. Madeline's first novel had been a finalist for the PEN-Faulkner Award.

Suddenly I felt shy of ever riding horses with Madeline; surely I would look such a farm girl. Our horse relationship had been a cerebral one, not an actual experience. I imagined myself on my potential purchase loping carelessly through a field, the dogs straining to catch up, the only music the birds and the wind. Nonfiction, even the elusive genre of creative nonfiction, depended on blunt prosaic reality that didn't necessarily provide the opportunity for perfect transformation. Had I overstated the metaphor? Still, was not the task the same: the writer, the words, the shift? Yes, that was it—it was that magical shift, not the gait itself.

Do you remember the horse?

Of course, I replied.

Do you remember, Bobbie, the times we went at midnight when the silver light slid through the hallway window and the black limbs of the front yard elm sketched cracks over the full moon's face? We had only one horse, so we rode bareback together. Surely our mother knew, but well aware of the significance of shared childhood secrets, she feigned sleep. Do you remember, Bobbie, the bridle bit we warmed in our hands, the creak of the icy gate, the cold squeak of the packed snow when the horse shifted magically into that smooth slow canter after we crossed the creek?

He had not answered. This happened the last time I saw him, when he had pneumonia and could barely speak. He opened his eyes when I thought he had already slipped into sleep.

Often we had good times as children, he said.

Chapter Four

The only irregularity, if it could be called that, of the memorial service for my brother in early June was the slightly belated and noisy appearance of two of our three half-sisters, Roberta and Betty, the offspring of our father's adventure with the schizophrenic Dorothy. I had been handing out the simple memorial bulletins and greeting people at the door, thanking them for coming. So many people came that I had run out of the printed programs, and when the women came through the church door, at first I didn't know who they were. Then I recognized Roberta, although her hair was no longer brown, but gray. I hugged both the half-sisters rather perfunctorily and thanked them for coming, but I was still trying to talk to the pastor to find out whether there were more programs to hand out. The half-sisters had been in a race against time, obviously, and must not have had time to change from their shorts. Actually, there were three women, one a sort of grown-up child who smiled pleasantly but didn't speak. This was very confusing, and I never got their names right until my nephew sorted it out for me later.

Not to nit-pick, Aunt Barbara, he said, but that was not Billie, it was Betty. Billie is your older half-sister who lives in Florida. I think the other woman who didn't speak belonged to Betty, and she was intellectually challenged.

I was ashamed of myself, and I admitted it to him right up front. I didn't even offer the excuse that I had been rather nervous and overwhelmed by the unexpected crowd.

I'd never even seen Betty, who had come from Kansas specifically for this occasion, except that one time in childhood when Dorothy's father Ben brought them to Sunday school at the Scotch Grove Presbyterian Church. Betty was a small woman, and it was to her side that the unexplained woman-child clung. When greeted, the rather pretty brown-haired woman held out a cell phone with a picture of Tinker-Bell on it. Betty's blue eyes were the only feature of our mutual father's family traits that I recognized.

I had not expected many people to come to the service—certainly none but relatives and the still ambulatory church members who remembered us and were loyal to our mother's memory. The *Monticello Express* had botched the announcement I e-mailed them, publishing the service with a name no one would have recognized at all, so I figured that even those who might have been interested would hear about the memorial service only by chance. But somehow they all knew. The church pews were almost full of kindly and curious people; classmates, cousins, even Marge, the one who sent the fruit baskets to my brother, had come all the way from Indiana. Thank god I'd bought the bigger cake at Family Foods, and the church ladies had come through with Jell-O desserts and brownies. We're so glad you're doing this for Bobbie, more than one person said to me; he was such a nice young man.

At first I advised the pastor that thirty bulletins would surely be enough, but the minimum order was sixty. We had been spared the usual farmer/tractor scene on the front of it—instead, a river wound across a meadow and disappeared in the distance. I liked that picture—I was surely into river metaphors now—and I was sorry to be empty handed with no more to give away. Whoever would have imagined such a crowd in this scattered, rural community for a man who disappeared under questionable circumstances thirty years ago?

It was well past time for the service to begin, and I could see that the pastor was trying to quiet things down. The problem was that the half-sisters had headed for my nephews' families in the front pews, and they were busy introducing themselves to everyone, explaining how they fit into the family. This was touching to me, although somewhat inconvenient, and I felt an unexpected surge of sympathy and affection. I had the ridiculous thought of announcing to the now seated congregation that these girls were left in an orphanage, you know, and after all, we were all just children. I could see that I was needed so I went forward and gently touched Roberta's shoulder. "The pastor's trying to begin the service," I said, and the women quickly and apologetically sat down in the pews behind the nephews. I returned to the fourth pew from the back on the right-hand side of the church, where my brother and I had always sat with our mother.

The soloist, though obviously unfamiliar with the old hymn I had requested, had a nice voice. The tinny piano was slightly distracting, the organ more mellow, and at my request, we didn't sing *The Old Rugged Cross,* which always made me remember how the congregation slowed down until everyone was rocking slightly. The pastor, an energetic, rather dramatic woman whose talent for delivery surely deserved much more of an audience than this rural church could provide, elaborated on the written text I had given her about my brother's life with well-chosen Bible passages and the usual assurances that, however imperfect anyone was, heaven could be achieved if he or she believed. When the pastor asked others to share positive memories, our cousin Dee, who lived up the road from us as a child and was more of a sister to me than a cousin, told a charming story about a time the three of us had camped out in the yard and the cat had kittens on our blankets.

Then my brother's son, the older one with the unfortunate family name of Robert, went to the podium and spoke. This young man was positively beautiful, with the Clark height and white hair that he wore shoulder length. He reminded me slightly of the picture of Jesus from the community funeral home calendar that hung in my brother's bedroom when he was a child. I had earlier explained to all the cousins, some whom I was seeing for the first time in many years, how I had gotten to know my nephew Bob quite well over the last two-and-a-half years since I'd located my brother.

I knew the younger son Bill less well because he was not given to verbose e-mails, but he was equally the responsible family man and was awfully nice as well. I was anxious that Bill not feel obligated to give any public testimonial as he had been younger when his father disappeared and frankly, he confided, barely remembered him at all. Bill especially endeared himself to me when he leaned over and whispered, as we walked to the cemetery after the service, and the half-sisters were talking to anyone who would listen, "There's a story there, for sure." I hugged him; perhaps this young man would understand my complicated feelings about these women for whom I felt such reserve when they were trying so hard to be supportive and kind.

Son Bob held both the curious and the caring in his sway with his extemporaneous speech. He was a natural speaker with a compelling but conversational voice, and his religious sincerity was obvious but not overbearing. He talked about his relationship with his mostly absent father, his understanding of alcoholism and his father's struggle for sobriety, his belief in God's wisdom, and a conversation he had with his father, shortly before the end of his life when he finally saw him again. His father had assured him that the painful condition of his body was a result of the way he had lived his life, his payment for his sins, and the pain would be relieved in heaven. Bobbie had also assured his son that he read the Bible every day and believed.

How interesting, amazing, in fact, I thought, as I listened, positively spellbound, to my nephew. I had heard nothing about this sincere faith from my brother. This must have happened when the grandchildren had been taken for the Florida visit. I had seen mostly exhibitions of the behavior and verbalizations from Bobbie that the hospital staff assured me were responsible for his psychotic diagnosis.

Therefore, the son said in closing, because of his own and his father's belief, he did not mourn a physical death that relieved such earthly torment. He knew that his father was now in heaven and had escaped at last the curse of his addiction and the physical pain of his body.

Those assembled in the church gave a collective sigh of relief, except for me, the baffled but grateful sister. I simply smiled through my tears at my nephew and felt glad that my brother had managed such a coherent conversation to comfort his son for the impending loss of a father he never really had.

Could it be, I thought later when walking on the beach at home again, that this elder son had achieved what had seemed impossible to me even in Nepal; that he had performed the required ceremony to usher the father to heaven? I would have loved to discuss this with Eloise.

The surprise of the service, however, was the grandson, little six-year-old Ben, whose bright blue eyes and dark curls combined to create a startling resemblance to his grandfather as a child. "Why that little boy is a spittin' image of Bobbie," one elderly cousin who had been close to Eloise repeated over and over, shaking her head. Ben came to the pulpit uncoached to stand beside his father. The congregation sat spellbound and silent, and the brave little boy spoke clearly so everyone could hear him.

"I'm sorry that I will not know my grandpa, and I hope he is in heaven with God."

This time there was a collective intake of breath. Even the pastor choked up on the spontaneous statement from such a beautiful child.

After a long minute it was obvious that no one was going to try to compete with that performance, so I stood up and spoke from the pew where our mother had placed us every Sunday of our childhood. I thanked all the people who had helped me with the service, especially my cousin Dee, who had organized the fellowship hour before I came from Oregon. I also thanked the relatives who had baffled me by making a point of telling me that they were praying for my soul.

The next surprise came as the pastor stepped up to conclude the service. My brother's ex-wife Karen, who had been discharged from the hospital for pneumonia the previous day and looked genuinely ill, stood up and walked in an alarmingly uncertain gait to the pulpit. The congregation stared at Karen in blank curiosity; thirty years ago she had been blamed in the community for the divorce and maybe even for her then husband's descent into alcoholism.

I was once married in this church, Karen began, but it was many years, even lifetimes, ago. I recognize some of your faces, although several members of the congregation who knew me and who were beloved by the man I married then, and whose memory we honor today, have already passed on.

It was extremely important, especially in a memorial service like this, Karen said, to acknowledge that there was much more to the lives of individuals so afflicted than the chemical addiction that had led them into unrecognizable behaviors. It was essential to give credit to the sum total of a person's existence. She knew that it was unusual for an ex-wife to give a glowing testimonial for a former husband, but she wanted the community to know what a good citizen Bob had been and that he had loved his family. They might not be aware that even though he was absent during his sons' adolescence that he had been a responsible father by setting aside money for his sons' care and education from the sale of land he had inherited. He was, she said, both a good man and a good Christian, and after enumerating several examples, such as his participation in politics and his faithful church attendance, Karen somewhat shakily sat down.

Touched by the simple truth and kindness of Karen's statement, I bowed my head. I thought of Candy and the Naked-Red-Girl; I had been guilty of judging my brother, of declaring his life meaningless because of my own terms. "Judge not," I said silently, repeating a verse that had once gained me a gold star on the Sunday school room wall, "that ye be not judged." The pastor regained the pulpit and complimented Karen on her unusual generosity toward an ex-spouse.

"I have not heard that kind of testimonial from an ex-spouse before," the pastor said, smiling directly at Karen. "That was a brave and valuable contribution, and I commend you for it." Then the pastor proceeded to close the service. Skillfully, with careful elocution, she read the eulogy I had written for my brother, which harkened back to the image of a child peering into the darkened barn, looking for his father. The eulogy, which depended on an understanding of family background and a tangle of repeated names and references to financial failings to make much sense to the congregation, was met with the same blank curiosity as Karen's speech. I did not mind that, as the lines had not been written for the congregation, anyway. It was my personal expression of absolution for us all; all of our lives, however they were judged by others, had meaning. At last I understood the link of loneliness and loss for the fathers and the sons; perhaps even the loneliness and loss for the daughters, even though at the time I had written the piece, it was not for them I had penned the lines in my notebook.

My brother Bobbie had bright blue eyes and a cowlick on the right side of his forehead; he was a child who made his own reality. When told about Santa Claus, he refused to believe it. "There is a big man, a very big man," he insisted. "He brings all the presents." What began as slight variations of facts grew to bear little resemblance to what qualified as truth.

Bobbie knew about truth. As a child he went every Sunday with his mother and sister to the Scotch Grove Presbyterian Church. But he made true in his mind what he needed to believe. "My daddy is milking the cows in the barn," he insisted to my mother after our father had left the family. "No, Bobbie, your daddy is gone," our mother said gently; "the cows are gone, too."

When grown, he wanted to be the big man who brought all the presents to family and friends. But he clung to the door of the darkened barn, still seeking his absent father. He succeeded too well in his task, becoming himself the father he had wanted to find, leaving the sons he had so loved. In the lives of ordinary individuals, chemical addiction is a family tragedy of degradation and shame. Not for us the lucrative entertainment of celebrities who enter expensive clinics under the fascinated gaze of adoring fans, but missed birthdays and baseball games, lonely Christmas mornings. (Bobbie and Billie, your daddy is gone; the cows are gone, too.)

But today, let us remember together a young man with bright blue eyes and a slight cowlick on the right side of his forehead. His later all-too-familiar human failures do not negate his earlier contributions: his service to his country, his fine young sons. He was a man who came to church every Sunday of his young life, and loved his family and friends.

The pastor led the singing of the last hymn with considerable gusto, and when it was finished, she gave the benediction and invited all to a fellowship hour in the church basement.

Buffered by bakery cake and Hawaiian Punch, we all congratulated ourselves and each other on such a lovely service; several people remarked to me that it was the best funeral they had been to in a long time. Cousin Marge took picture after picture, lining up the aging cousins in a row against the gray cement wall of the church basement just to the left of a silenced humidifier.

I looked around at relatives and community members fondly. What a surprising release this whole memorial service had provided: the chance for my nephews and all the rest of us to come to some kind of closure, the positive feeling generated for my brother, the provision of a quasi-redemption for one who left family, church, and community under an unfortunate alcoholic cloud. God bless the Iowa small towns and the Presbyterians, I thought humbly; my brother and I were lucky to grow up where and when we did.

Many people, both family and those with their own dead relatives there, walked the short distance to the Scotch Grove cemetery, even though there was no body to follow and only the inscription to my brother's memory that I had placed on my mother's stone to see. "Buried at Sea," had been engraved under the name and dates. Finally I attended to Eloise's family stone, too, and I pointed it out to my nephews along with the stones of other family ancestors. They listened and looked politely. "The first woman elder in the Scotch Grove Presbyterian Church," the inscription for Eloise read.

Once again, the pastor, who sensed my rather dazed ambivalence, intervened to relieve me from the attention of the well-meaning half-sisters, and I walked back to the church with my nephews. Six-year-old Ben and I looked for frogs in the pond that had formed by the road in last night's thunderstorm. After the church basement was again tidy, and the humidifier was humming, I returned to the old farmhouse to sit at the kitchen table with my cousin Vaneta, who no longer ran Sweet Memories as a Bed and Breakfast. We sorted out which cousins and women of the church looked more or less antique than we did.

Later, I strolled slowly through the amber Iowa evening on the barely maintained, enter-at-your-own-risk gravel road that stretched for a mile and a half from the farmhouse of my childhood to the church. I stopped for pictures of certain flowers in the Scotch Grove Prairie, that land that the Jones County Conservation Commission, much to Eloise's disapproval, had carefully restored to wildness, and I tried unsuccessfully to locate in the leaves of an old cottonwood a common yellowthroat's black-masked form.

On the final approach to the church building itself, I walked through the cemetery and stopped at my mother's stone, reading once more the inscription I had engraved for my brother. A little romantic, I thought, for what was no doubt a group disposal of remains leftover from research (once every six months we do it, the woman at MedCure informed me), but I liked it nonetheless. "And you didn't even need a fog canoe, Bobbie," I said aloud, as if we were standing together reading it, "like the natives of Wapato Island." Even though there wasn't one ash flake of what had been my brother there, I summarized aloud for him his memorial service, the nice things his family had said about his life having meaning, and I repeated verbatim the words of little Ben.

I couldn't undo those empty years or recreate the fierce child-hood love, even though I understood now that it was my willful ignorance of addiction that led me to fail him when he needed me most. Not that I could have saved him, but I could have helped him save himself with my affirming love and emotional presence. I'm not sure why I didn't say that aloud because it would have explained my absence, except that we had never talked of personal things.

"It was good that I finally came, Bobbie," was the best I could muster. And I repeated the last words I heard him say. "Often we had good times as children." My mother would like to hear that, too, I decided.

By the time I reached the church, it was only a blank silhouette at the edge of a fractured, golden disk. This perfect prairie sunset would make a dandy funeral bulletin, I thought suddenly. I imagined a little pamphlet like we'd had for my brother's service, the one with the river flowing through the meadow, only mine would have a picture of the small church against the expanse of purple sky, suggesting humbly one potential for spiritual meaning within the enormity of the universe. Now what pithy little saying would I put inside this funeral bulletin to communicate to the congregation what I had learned of life and death?

A line from the Bible? I might not be a true believer, but the church had undisputedly influenced my life. I sighed, shifting my weight from one leg to the other. This was harder than I thought. Finally I sat down on the steps of the church and took out the

Nude Beach Notebook, flipping it open quickly so no disapprov-
ing Presbyterian spiritual force the church harbored would think
ill of me for the racy title on the cover. What had I learned, really?
I opened to a blank page:

Life.

I wrote that one word and underlined it.
I had learned that life, though beautiful and perhaps "enough,"
was fragile and fraught with elusive meaning.

Death.

And as for death, I had learned nothing conclusive. Death,
for all the theories that have held the imaginations of cultures
and defined powerful religions, retained its mystery.
Nothing in that for a funeral bulletin.
Then I thought of the nude woman in the Gilbert River, the
girl with the golden skin, the dark hair, and the cranes that flew
low over my head, reminding me of my own mortality. I remembered what I had felt when I considered Lucretius and his theory
of the recombination of atoms as I lay in the grass. I am that I
am. That was from the Bible.

I am that I am.

Yes, that would do, I thought as I wrote the phrase in my
notebook. I didn't mean just me. We are what we are, and while
we may not know the meaning of life, all of our lives are meaningful.

Life goes too fast.

One mystery remained, and it still troubled me when I
returned home to walk again on the beach by the Columbia River.
Why had my soul become a focal point for kindly family concern?
I had made no particular announcement of a disagreement with
conventional Christian beliefs, of my ecumenical acceptance of all
religions as cultural expressions bubbling from a common spring,

or of my wishy-washy agnosticism. Did I have the mark of Cain on my forehead for ignoring my brother's plight for so long?

No one said so, certainly not my cousin Vaneta, who had consistently urged me to find Bobbie, calling to mind the implied Biblical injunction to be my brother's keeper. In the summer we had spent together while I was doing research for an earlier book, *Prairie Reunion,* Vaneta had scolded me for not going to church, but now she admitted that she had not attended services herself the past year except for funerals. Every Sunday my cousin and her husband, both in precarious health and hard of hearing, which made the church setting somewhat uncomfortable, put their dog in the car and drove the forty miles to Dubuque to check on the Mississippi. "It feels good," Vaneta said, "for us to just sit there with the dog, watching the river."

I could certainly relate to that.

Chapter Five

Each spring, the people who control the dams release levers some-where and our world changes at the moorage as the water beneath us rises. The river turns from its soft green hue to a much more menacing brown, laced with debris. Large logs with root balls that have previously been on dry land come floating down the Channel, and gulls and herons sit on them for a free ride. The bridge that connects the boardwalk to the riverbank shifts from its uphill slant until it is almost level. This usually happens in May, but the year of my brother's memorial service, it continued clear into late June because of the heavy spring rains and record snowpack in the mountains. We all began somewhat nervously to wonder whether the parking lot would flood like it did in 1996, when all the cars had to be moved to higher ground.

Our houseboats, floating homes as they were now called in real-estate brochures, the terminology change reflecting a new sophistication or at least higher prices associated with the river way of life, were not threatened this time, but they had been in the hundred-year-flood of 1996. There was simply too much rain and snowmelt all at once to allow a controlled flow, and those who had been at Mayfair then had impressive stories to tell. "The whole kit and caboodle woulda floated down the river if tug-boats hadn't been called in to hold the boardwalk in place," Mike Denny had said right after we moved to the moorage in 1999. He had marked on one of the pilings how high the water had been during the flood. "See right there," he said, pointing to a painted line on the large permanent pipes where he had put a gauge. "We went up that high, and the parking lot was completely under-water. You could see Mount Hood from your house 'cause we were level with the top of the dike. I took people to their cars in my boat. When the water reaches eighteen on the gauge, you're going to lose your wood pile and anything else in the parking lot, so you'd better get your cars moved in time." After that flood, new metal pilings had been installed.

This element of impermanence intrigued me. The moorages along the Willamette's seventeen-mile Multnomah Channel, which empties into the Columbia at the end of the island, seemed almost like the native villages that once were here. In the summer on the strip of muddy shore along Burlington Bottoms, the wet-land directly across from my study window, I've occasionally seen illegal artifact hunters. What artifacts will remain when our house-boats finally float downstream? I've heard dark tales of what early moorage residents shoved overboard before stringent regulations were in place. The rusting hull of Lorraine's car that floated away in '96 can still be seen in the swamp beyond the parking lot. "We couldn't get it moved out before the water came," Mike Denny said. "No way that car was going to start. It had sat there for a couple of years after they took away her license for drivin' drunk."

The year of my brother's memorial, however, the flow crested at 17.6, and the seepage from the swamp on the other side of the parking lot, which had been creeping toward the woodpiles, lev-eled. For me, however, the problem was the Columbia River on the other side of the island. It had all but obliterated the beaches for a month, and when I left for Iowa and my brother's memorial service, my fervent hope was that the sand would have emerged by the time I came back. The situation had been difficult to explain to the dogs. Each morning I faced their unhappy faces when we turned toward Wapato Park where leashes were necessary so no wildlife would be disturbed. Surely, I promised them, by the time I returned, the water would have receded and at least part of the Nude Beach would be again available for a morning run.

Except it wasn't. When I came home the gauge was still at seventeen, and the bridge to the mainland was flat. All that snow-melt in Canada had to go somewhere, and here it was right on the Nude Beach and Willow Bar. Even the beach at the beginning of the trail to Warrior Rock had only a sliver of sand. The only possibility for a dog run was the upper bench on the Social Security Beach dike, but I didn't want another skunk encounter, and fishermen were out there in full force at first light.

Devi chewed up an entire pillow, and Pani ate a sock and ripped up a pair of Jim's shorts. I can't help it, dogs, I said to their disappointed whines every time I turned the wrong way in the morning, taking them to the state park where they remained on their leashes. Sometimes, even in the morning, I drove over the island bridge to Forest Park. As soon as the gauge dropped a foot, I gave in, and early one morning we headed for the Columbia. Devi warbled happily in anticipation, and Pani barked right in my ear all the way across the island. I didn't sing, though, because I didn't have hope of much exposed sand, if there was any at all, and if I sang the dogs would get even more excited. Maybe they could eke out a short beach run at the beginning of the Warrior Rock trail.

At the Nude Beach no sand at all was exposed at my customary entrance, the one for normal-people-who-just-like-to-take-off-their-clothes. The dogs and I stared forlornly where the dirty water still lapped at the road, not deep but over my boot tops. "I'll try downstream," I said aloud to the dogs, as there was a high loaf of dredged sand farther along that would surely be out of water if we could reach it on the path. Sure enough, there was a pick-up truck parked against the fence on the other side of the road. I was surprised to see the truck this early in the morning, but if someone was parked there, surely there must be at least a stretch of beach accessible. Maybe another houseboat resident desperate to run dogs, I thought. "I'll check this out and be right back," I said aloud, and the dogs peered impatiently out the back window of the car.

If I had not so raised their expectations, I'd have given up and gone back to the lake below the moorage. I didn't want to, however, as the mosquitoes attacked ravenously there, and the tall wet pollen-laden grass arched across the path, making my throat swell. The mosquitoes were equally ravenous along the Columbia, I realized when I entered the trees. The beginning of the slightly elevated path was dry, but ahead I could see the silver shine of water across it. Perhaps it wasn't deep, and the person with the pick-up had waded through it.

Except he hadn't.

I realized that when I heard a movement in the nettles to my left. A man was standing there, a man who was absolutely buck naked except that his body was entirely covered in tattoos: snakes, a large red devil face, monster figures. He was pudgy, and his hair stood up wildly. Mosquitoes surrounded him in a swarm, and he began to pump his arms. He smiled broadly and thrust out his crotch.

My god, it, too, sported a tattoo—at the end of his waving member there was a little smiley face.

Didn't it *hurt* when they put that on? I didn't know anything about tattoos; maybe it wasn't a real tattoo.

My second thought was that the man must have stepped off the path to relieve himself. But in the nude? In mosquitoes and nettles? I began to back up as he stepped forward. "Excuse me," I said, "I only wanted to run my dogs on the sand." I backed up more, and he stepped forward again, pumping his crotch.

Should I run for the car? I didn't want to turn my back to him and appear overly frightened. There were so many mosquitoes attacking my face and wrists that I couldn't think straight. If I had brought the dogs with me, would they have protected me or would one of them have simply stuck her nose up this man's butt? I'd never had dogs that were as rude as these pups. Inappropriately, in spite of my fear, I felt like laughing.

Stepping backward, I zigged where I should have zagged and almost fell off the elevated track of the path. Surely I was close to the sign at the entrance; I had barely started toward the sand. My mind slowed down, wandered off, in fact, into irrelevancy. Clothing optional, the sign would say, so this tattooed crotch-pumper was perfectly legal, certainly more legal than I would have been had I brought the dogs off their leashes. Was this the same entrance where in mid-winter I had seen the man in the fishnet stockings?

The fishnet-stocking morning I had hiked with the dogs to the lighthouse at Warrior Point, the place where Captain Broughten had been met with the elaborately carved canoes. Thirty-seven degrees, I had told my husband later, and the river had white caps. The young man who was scuttling across the road toward the beach wore only a garter belt, fishnet stockings, and combat boots.

"In this wind?" Jim had scoffed. "He'll be lucky if he doesn't lose his pecker to frost-bite."

Thinking of Jim's remark, I did laugh, more of a high-pitched nervous squawk. Today's even less-clothed subject was in serious jeopardy of a similar sacrifice to mosquitoes, and I imagined a frown on the collapsed smiley face. I had reached the road so I wheeled and bolted for the car, quickly locking the doors behind me. Now I had only the disappointed whine of the dogs to deal with. The tattooed man had stopped his advance at the gravel; in fact, he had disappeared altogether.

I drove away slowly, not wanting this man to know he had been so successful in frightening me. But he had, my idyllic morning Eden of beautiful clouds and light transformed by a man with devil tattoos, I thought angrily. And it wasn't just him despoiling the scene. Debris that had been flung behind trees by last season's revelers, and worse yet, discarded oil from past generations careless dumping, now loosed by the flood of the spring runoff, floated on water that lapped at the road. Lines from Gerard Manley Hopkins came to mind:

Generations have trod, have trod, have trod;
  And all is seared with trade; bleared, smeared with toil;
  And wears man's smudge and shares man's smell . . .

What a mess we had made of this place of such exquisite beauty. How could we ever clean it up?

As the road rose to the top of the dike, I left the oil behind and could see across the mighty Columbia. The dogs had given up hope and settled in the back of the car. My heartbeat had now slowed to a somewhat normal rate, and I took a few deep breaths. Heavy clouds that hovered just above the horizon began to break and caught the rising sun on their bright bellies, casting a warm brownish light over the swollen river and turning every pond on the waterlogged island gold. I thought again of Hopkins.

And for all this, nature is never spent;
  There lives the dearest freshness deep down things;

I pulled over to the side of the road and, after glancing in the rearview mirror to make sure no pickup truck was in sight, I pulled out my notebook. With a little help from the poet, I could refuse to give this ugly incident power to spoil the beauty of the island morning for me. Once I had known his poem by heart, and I wrote the remembered phrases in my notebook.

My mother had loved Hopkins because he used nature to reflect her own religious feelings, and she had quoted the ending to me at another sunrise some fifty years ago: "Because the Holy Ghost over the bent / World broods with warm breast and with ah! bright wings."

                        ᔥ

For several days after my unexpected meeting with the Man-with-the-Devil-Tattoo, I walked my properly leashed dogs around the trail at Wapato Park rather than even try to go to the Nude Beach. Not that I was afraid, I told myself; it had, after all, been a chance meeting with this strange, threatening man, but

I had to wait for the water to recede anyway. There was no purpose served by reporting him to the Fish and Wildlife authorities, the agency actually in charge of that whole end of the island. More of the wildlife, they might say with a chuckle. They probably thought that I, with my daily pre-dawn and sometime winter afternoon pilgrimages, was equally odd.

The whole thing sounded so unbelievable—why would anyone stand nude in the middle of the brush and nettles with all those mosquitoes? Even if I omitted the details like the monster-devil figure that covered his entire abdomen or the smiley face, they might think I was making this up; and they might turn on me as a troublemaker who compromised their rules by running my dogs off-leash at the beach. I minimized the frightening aspects of the encounter when I summarized it for Jim. "That must have been one of those plastic stickers," Jim had said of the smiley face, "or he used a magic marker of sorts. You can bet it wasn't a real tattoo, not *there*, for sure."

But I wished that the whole thing had never happened. For me, the Nude Beach was an early morning Eden with mists and crane calls that hinted at immortality, and I preferred to think of the Odd Ones I encountered as harmless and perhaps misunderstood eccentrics. That morning, safely back at the houseboat, I had flipped through my notes of the previous winter: I was not the only one who had described the island in idyllic terms. I had paraphrased a passage from the journal of Alexander Ross.

Alexander Ross of an Astor Expedition in 1811 observed that natives here seemed to have an abundance of food, time for festivities such as horse racing—the tracks still visible as of his writing, swimming and canoe racing, berry gathering, gambling games and trading fairs. The natives experienced a "degree of happiness" seldom exhibited among "civilized" men who were beset with greater anxieties. So our island seems to have been a veritable paradise with a few inconsistencies; there were too many fleas, for one thing, and some slaves. Among the slaves of particular interest to the Astor party were some Canadian employees who had deserted their own company and had been captured as they were making their way home. They were freed and returned to the Astor Expedition exploratory party in trade for eight blankets and a brass kettle.

This notebook business was definitely getting out of hand, I thought in annoyance as a sheaf of papers, mostly paraphrases of historical sources and online journals that I had stuck between the pages, fell onto the floor. Some sheets, I noted, were e-mails I had copied when I was going back and forth to Florida to see my brother. I gathered them up in a cardboard box, not even bothering for any sort of order. I should probably dump the notebook in there, too, I thought, as it was the synthesizing factor in this random assortment of notes: descriptions of island scenery and history, memories of childhood, the painful reconciliation with my brother. The notebook and the Nude Beach: that was where it had come together for me, a certain peace from this collage of past, present, and place. Only a few blank pages in between entries were left. Time for a new notebook, I told myself, but out of habit I stuffed the slimmed down version back into my pack.

The dogs were restless and chased each other around the house. Finally the computer chart showed the water level in the river falling, and our moorage ramp to the bank began to slant at a more familiar angle. Perhaps I could walk the path on my usual Nude Beach entrance now and at least continue a short way down the sand. In the late afternoon when the tide was full out, we would go and try again, I decided.

The weather had turned uncommonly chilly and blustery for late June, and showers were forecast all day. Inclement weather suited me just fine; there was always the chance that the sun would break through later. Any available beach would be sparsely populated at best. In fact, when I arrived mid-afternoon, no cars at all were parked at my usual entrance, although I couldn't see around the curve to parking spaces by other paths. A large pond still filled most of the pasture on the west side of the road. How unusual this was so late in the year; normally Fish and Wildlife cattle would be grazing there. In the winter I had seen much bird life on the shallow silver plate: widgeon, pintails, even teal, and sometimes snow geese. For about a week in the spring, cranes were feeding along the edge, practicing their long-legged dance before the migration. No ducks on the water now, but six white egrets stood on the other side, their reflections wrinkled by the wind. I should have brought my camera.

Even with the tide full out, I had to cross barely drained mud in the swale along the road, and there were only a few hundred yards of sand for the dogs to run before a wide arm of water separated us from another lobe of the beach. Small human figures walked there, too, obviously having gained access by another path, but I didn't distinguish anyone familiar. No Big Indian; he had mentioned the last time I saw him that he was leaving on a road trip, maybe to return to his Cherokee family. No Naked-Red-Girl, no String-Can-Man, and, thankfully, no Man-With-the-Devil-Tattoo. The water would be well over my boot tops were I to cross the full canal between the more elevated mounds of sand, so after a few times up and down the available length of beach, I sat down on a wet log while the dogs wrestled and dug, with Devi taking occasional short forays after low-flying gulls.

This sunshine would not last for long; in fact, a squall was moving in from the north, obliterating the small white Warrior Rock lighthouse at the curved downstream island tip. Tomorrow I would hike down there in the morning with the dogs, not on the beach of course, which would still be underwater, but on the old road that wound its way through the trees. I had hiked there often, fascinated by the bony spine of rocks, the remains of an old wooden boat factory at the very tip, where the Multnomah Channel of the Willamette on which our houseboat was moored joined with the Columbia River. Exactly where had the highly decorated warrior canoes, with their intricately decorated headboards, waited for Lt. Broughten? Probably not in our Multnomah Channel, but out in the Columbia itself. Where, I wondered each time, had the natives placed the burial canoes waiting for high water? Were they on stilts to escape animal carnage or were they all, like the one that the naturalist Townsend had plundered, hung in trees? I imagined the forlorn brother, following the telltale tracks on the sand that established the thief of his sister's body as a white man. How pivotal that story from the island past had been in my own resolution of family responsibility.

The computer chart showed the river lowering drastically in the next two weeks as the ones who controlled the dams cut the snowmelt flow to fill reservoirs, so soon the dogs and I would be back to our normal routine. Even this brief time on the beach today had helped us all, but it appeared that we were going to get thoroughly drenched if we didn't head back to the car. I stood up to look for the dogs when they did not appear with my usual call. Where were they, anyway? I fumbled in my pocket for the whistle before I saw them. They had stopped playing and were at the downstream edge of the available land among the dark Oregon ash trees, staring intently across the wide canal of floodwater that still separated them from the next promising loaf of sand.

When Pani began her friendly bark, and Devi yodeled her strange vocalization that sounded like a human greeting, it was obvious that they knew the man approaching on the other side of the water. Then I, too, recognized the Builder's shaggy white hair. He raised the pole he was carrying in greeting, so I threaded through the young Oregon ash trees that stood with their feet in water at the edge of our sand peninsula. The Builder was not nude like one pink figure I had seen in the distance earlier, but his shirt was off and tied around his waist. Yes, that was exactly as I had wanted my brother to look when I found him. Tall and straight like he had been when I knew him, not curled up in a painful fetal position, unable to straighten his legs.

The Builder must have used the gay men's entrance path to get to that loaf of sand, I decided, or maybe the transvestite entrance. No doubt the straight pole he was carrying was for another lean-to, as it was the typical length of ones he chose. "Are you waiting for the wind?" I called. He couldn't hear me and cupped one hand behind his ear. "Wind," I shouted this time and pointed at the squall that was moving upstream and would descend on us both in another minute. He still didn't seem to hear, so I just waved to acknowledge him, and he held up his pole.

"Too long," he called, and his voice carried because the wind was blowing my direction. He waited to see if I had heard. I nodded and waved. He called again. "Too long."

Now how odd was *that*? The Builder never talked about anything but the wind. He may have meant that the beach whitened pole he'd found was too long for the lean-to he was building, or maybe that the high water had gone on too long, but I caught my breath. Wasn't that what my brother had said when he saw me for the first time in Orlando? The thought made me dizzy. I remembered his words specifically because they had raised such ambivalent feelings for me; my love almost choked by the resentment of what seemed then to be his self-inflicted miserable condition.

It was going to rain hard. My jeans, my hair, the dogs, even the notebook would be soaked, so I tucked it inside my shirt. So much water everywhere. "*Life flows like water,*" I thought. The line from Jean Anouilh had gone through my mind in the nursing home, and it surfaced again as I faced the approaching squall. The wind slammed hard, and the Builder and I turned away from each other when the rain, passing rapidly upriver, hit in a silver sheet. When I raised my head, the Builder had already gone; how did he disappear so quickly, and where did he go?

But wasn't that what my brother had said?

My mind whirled like the squall around me. Surely this was just coincidental, wasn't it? Not an Eloise-type miracle, not a sign of anything magical, not a communication from beyond the watery grave of what remained of my brother's ashes once the research people were done. I tried to hold my mind in check because once one started down that symbolic path of coincidental occurrences—separation by water, those on the other side—there was no end to the miracles that could be strung together to justify a belief in some kind of afterlife. On that point I surely had remained a skeptic at best, but it brought a surge of something akin to joy that after all my ruminations, death had remained an unexplained transformation, a resilient mystery.

The rain slashed, and even the dogs turned against it as we walked toward the car. I had held emotion carefully at bay, but now it broke from inside me like the squall itself. For the first time, really, since Bobbie had died, I let myself feel the full force of loss for us all. *Life flows like water through our hands.*

I loaded the dogs in the car and sat there watching the egrets standing tall in the rain.

"Too long." Was that really what my brother had said?

Yes, it was, it definitely was, and I had the notebook to prove it.

"You've been gone too long."

Acknowledgements

A few names have been changed in this narrative to protect privacy.

I wish to thank my editors, Tom Booth and Micki Reaman at OSU Press, for their faith and perseverance through my successive versions of this manuscript.

Bette Husted, Andrea Carlisle, and Molly Gloss were invaluable in the composition of this narrative and I am thankful for their critical comments and suggestions for revision.

Relatives who provided helpful material and input include my nephews Bob and Bill Norris, Karen Sallis, and cousins Marge Phillips, Dee Rohrbacher, and Vaneta Luce. Eloise Sutherland Helgens, now deceased, contributed immeasurably to both this manuscript and my life.

Friends to whom I owe much for reading drafts and listening to my ruminations are Jean MacDonald, Eileen McVicker, Judy Wilder, Jane Edwards Nottberg, Patty Denny, Karen Hancock and Julia Bergren.

I am exceedingly grateful to Tami Elswick for the years of love and family companionship that she afforded my brother.

Additionally, I would like to thank all readers of *The Nude Beach Notebook* for sharing my life.

The author gratefully acknowledges permission to include short excerpts from her earlier published works—*The Violet Shyness of Their Eyes: Notes from Nepal* (Calyx Books, 1993) and *Prairie Reunion* (Farrar, Straus and Giroux, 1995)—and excerpts from *Narrative of a Journey: Across the Rocky Mountains to the Columbia River* by John Kirk Townsend (OSU Press, 1999).

Other sources that provided valuable historical background include *Wappato Indians* and *Wappato Indians of the Lower Columbia River Valley* by Roy Franklin Jones (both privately printed); *Exile in the Wilderness* by Jean Murray Cole (University of Washington Press, 1979); *Chinook Texts* by Frank Boas (Bureau of American Ethnology, Government Printing Office, 1894); and The Journals of the Lewis and Clark Expedition (http://www.lewisandclarkjournals.unl.edu).